# STOLEN
# *Dance*

## An Olympian's Perpetual Search for Healing from Trauma and Grief

# STACIANA WINFIELD

Stolen Dance

An Olympian's Perpetual Search for Healing from Trauma and Grief

Staciana Winfield

Illustrations by Samantha Ramsden (Winfield)

ISBN (paperback): 978-1-962280-57-0
ISBN (ebook): 978-1-962280-58-7

*In loving memory of Brett Roderic Winfield*
*(April 24, 1979–December 22, 2016)*

May you feel the joy and strength of the water, stay grounded on this Earth, fly free through the air like a hummingbird, and spread your wings wide to serve others. May you find power in your voice, ignited by the breath of fire and a sense of belonging in this year of the dragon and beyond...

To Kyla,

Let's DANCE!

I love you forever...

-Mom-

# CONTENTS

# INTRODUCTION

*"[N]euroscience confirms that storytelling has the unique power to change opinions and behavior."*

—Luca Penati, quoted by
Wallace J. Nichols, Blue Mind[1]

My intention for this book is to increase my scope of positive impact and help others tap into the power of human connection through shared stories of adversity, as well as describing best practices for growing from grief and trauma. This book is inspired by many, but most specifically by the incredible power of positive psychology and the idea of *whakapapa*, which author Owen Eastwood describes in part as "being an enabler of a mindful approach to both performance and life."[2]

The power of collaboration has made this book better. As Brigadier General Rhonda Cornum said, "The enemy of good is better."[3] I felt the power of this book improve when

I shared it with people, and their feedback and willingness to contribute resources expanded the impact of the words on the page. I'm grateful for the shared consciousness and collective knowledge of humanity, as well as all the hours of research and dedication the humans represented in this book have dedicated during their lives to positively impact others. I hope you feel the energetic shift within you that this book has created within me.

This book is for a mature audience. It is full of sincere personal stories interwoven with themes of love and resilience, is supported by research-driven data, and includes adult language and explicit content that are a tribute to my authentic self. We wear many hats in our lives. As a child of teachers, I learned at an early age when it was inappropriate to swear. My mom's favorite word when my sister and I were little was "shit." As we grew older, it evolved to "fuck." My dad was worse. My sister found it funny at age three to jump on the bed while rhythmically shouting, "Bullshit! Bullshit! Bullshit!" and grinning from ear to ear in anticipation of my parents' reaction. She loved to get their attention by any means necessary. Mortified, my mom pointed at my dad and said, "Dane, you *know* this is your fault."

"Ha!" My dad chuckled and retorted, "That's bullshit!"

But my parents wouldn't dare show that side at school. They were raised by nuns in private Catholic schools in Cleveland.

They learned at an early age when to hide the foul language they picked up from the streets of a tough, urban city. My dad was kicked out of his Catholic high school for flipping off the camera in his senior picture. Ironically, later in life, he decided to become a teacher. He loved to learn; he just hated authority. He taught English, and my mom taught chemistry. Dinner table conversations were interesting.

My sister was the first one to encourage me to write a book. But the magnitude of permanence that a book embodies made me intimidated to write my story. When I was younger, I felt like my story wasn't finished yet. It seemed pretentious and narcissistic to write a memoir at age twenty. Eckhart Tolle has said, "Egoic intents are ones that feed the ego while non-egoic intents serve the greater good."[4] My intent for this book is based on my love for humanity and an experiential understanding of the human condition of trauma and grief. I've overcome enough adversity in the last four decades of my life to warrant a desire to share these stories with the intent to connect and help others thrive. Thanks to my daily mantra from the Lululemon Manifesto, "Do one thing a day that scares you,"[5] I'm leaning into the discomfort of vulnerability and the fear of not being able to control others' responses and judgments. If this book helps one person, I will be grateful. I hope that person is you.

I was afraid to write this book with my authentic voice. I have taught at private schools for over ten years. I may be judged for my language and my life. I owe infinite gratitude to Dr. Jeneen Graham, the current head of St. Margaret's Episcopal School, where I work, for her support and encouragement to all those she serves. Her willingness to read this book with a positive, critical-thinking lens about how to navigate others' responses moved me to tears—and showed me I could and should publish this book with an intent to serve.

And with humor, my sister continually reminded me through all my doubts, "Every parent reading this book at your school has a child, right?"

"Yes."

"Well, from experience, I can say with complete confidence that anyone who has a child has said a few swear words in their life. If they haven't, they're lying. They can handle it." She had a point.

Please just don't let your little ones read it. Thank you!

This "come with me" adventure is full of sincere stories from my own experience and perspective. I hope you connect with my vulnerability and my voice. I intend to make you laugh, cry, and feel all the feels, simultaneously. I hope you're willing to sit with the discomfort and read further. It will be worth it.

Since my midthirties, I have lived with a hole in my heart— an empty space, a void that brought me visceral pain. I'm in a club I never wanted to belong to, as a self-proclaimed member of The Hot Young Widows Club.[6] (I feel like author Nora McInerny and I could be best friends.) Through years of grief work, self-reflection, and authentic connection with others, I've learned to view the hole in my heart as a place of value. It's a place for expansion, to love and receive love in the space between—just like the value of a home is the empty space between the walls in which people can congregate, and the value of a window is the empty space inside the frame that allows the light to come in.[7] The space in my heart has value. It is filled with the Holy Spirit of community and oneness, which helps me channel the energy of others and radiates joy and love to those around me.

Owen Eastwood, a renowned performance coach, spent time uncovering the evolutionary story of *Homo sapiens* with Dr. Robin Dunbar, one of the world's leading evolutionary psychologists. In his book *Belonging*, Eastwood said of the experience, "[W]e mapped primal human needs that still direct us today: our need to belong converted into an emotive identity story; our need for a shared purpose transformed into a vision of the future; our need for shared beliefs to be translated into a code of how to behave."[8] My book is a testament to these primal needs and the importance of *whakapapa*, an ancient Māori code of togetherness, which I am grateful to have been taught through connections and conversation.

Eastwood explains the meaning behind *whakapapa*:

> Each of us are part of an unbreakable chain of people going back and forward in time. Back to our first ancestor at the beginning of time, and into the future to the end of time. Each of us in this chain of people have our arms interlocked with those on either side of us. We are unbreakable. Together immortal.
>
> The sun rose in the east and shone on our first ancestor. Here is our origin story. Just as happens with each passing day, the sun slowly moves down this unbreakable chain of people. Each of us will have our time in the sun. But the sun is always moving. Moving towards the west, where it will finally settle.
>
> When the sun shines on us we are alive, we are strong. For we have had passed down to us a culture that immerses us in deep belonging. We feel safe and respected. We share beliefs and a sense of identity with those around us and this anchors us. We shared a purpose with them. We share a vision of the future. We fit in here. Rituals and traditions tie us together. The experiences and wisdom of those who walked in the light before our time are passed on to us...When the sun is shining on us, we must be guardians of our tribe.[9]

I feel a strong sense of belonging and responsibility to this unbroken chain of human connection: to my family and the people who have experienced or will experience trauma and great loss. The definition of trauma, according to Dr. Paul Conti, is "any experience or experiences that modify our brain or neural circuitry...such that we do not function as well emotionally, behaviorally, or cognitively going forward from that experience."[10] We all have or will experience trauma, and I feel the need to share this sense of belonging to a larger group of people—to learn from the people of the past who are a part of the human condition, to increase connections and make an impact while the sun is shining on me, and to help those future people connected in this unbroken chain of togetherness that is the human condition.

If you are struggling with grief and trauma, I hope this book will inspire you to realize your connection to this unbroken chain of humanity. You are not alone. If you know someone who is struggling with grief and trauma, I hope you share this book with them. This book may be difficult to read in the beginning stages of grief, and if so, feel free to skip directly to part 5 to learn best practices for well-being.

If you are or were an athlete at any level and are struggling with the transition away from your sport, I hope you will read this book and recognize your place in the sun is just beginning. The stories here will shift your perspective of hardship and shine light on a shared purpose to thrive through daily living, which ultimately is the foundation of healing and growth. May this book give you the courage to share your stories, ask for and seek help, actively participate in best practices for well-being, and feel a deeper sense of connection to expand the space for all of us to grow together in strength, love, and light.

*"In your light I learn how to love. In your beauty, how to make poems. You dance inside my chest, where no one sees you, but sometimes I do, and that sight becomes this art."*

—Rumi[11]

# PROLOGUE

*"Now they've brought you away from here*
*I hope they didn't get your mind*
*Your heart is too strong anyway*
*We need to fetch back the time*
*They have stolen from us."*

—Milky Chance, "Stolen Dance"[12]

The night before my husband died, I found myself finally alone with him, and I had to dance. Holding his hand, attached to his comatose body, I needed him to know I was going to be okay. I was going to dance around him, celebrating our life and our forever love together. Led by my heart, not my head, I felt the warm joy of our marriage flow through me and into him. I listened to the lyrics of the music, and they too closely resembled the moment, like the song was about us:

"I want you by my side, so that I never have to be alone..."[13]

The tears streamed down my face.

"I hope they didn't get your mind, your heart is too strong anyway..."[14]

His heart continued to beat, but his communication had ceased. I knew his mind was still there, listening. More tears filled my eyes, and my chest constricted. I knew I had to fight the overwhelming feeling of grief, so I kept dancing through the tears. I wanted him to feel joy, peace, and love as his soul left his body. A stolen dance...on borrowed time.

# PART 1: WATER

*"Your heart is the size of an ocean. Go find yourself in its hidden depths."*

—Rumi[15]

# Only Breath

Not Christian or Jew or Muslim, not Hindu
Buddhist, Sufi, or Zen.
Not any religion or cultural system.
I am not from the East
or the West,
not out of the ocean
or up from the ground,
not natural or ethereal,
not composed of elements at all.
I do not exist,
am not an entity in this world
or in the next,
did not descend from Adam and Eve
or any origin story.
My place is placeless,
a trace of the traceless.
Neither body or soul.
I belong to the beloved,

have seen the two worlds as one
and that one call to and know,
first, last, outer, inner, only that
breath breathing human being.

—Rumi[16]

# Breathe

**Fall 1988, Age 7**

*I can't breathe, I can't breathe,* I thought, lying on the carpet, struggling to get air into my lungs.

"Judy, she's not breathing! SHE'S NOT BREATHING!" my dad yelled frantically to my mom.

"Okay, Dane," she responded, trying to calm him down. "We have to go."

My dad picked up my small seven-year-old body and put me in the car with my mom in the back seat. My ten-year-old sister, Alisha, sat with us, worried and scared. My mom looked down at my face and thought, *Her lips are blue.*

We lived only a few miles from the hospital in Leucadia, California, and we had fast freeway access from our neighborhood, Tortilla Flats. When nothing was wrong, my father was crazed, overprotective, and paranoid. Yet ironically, he would become calm and collected Superdad when a true crisis arose. He sped down the freeway like a superhero, living his worst nightmare. My parents and sister had watched me struggle to breathe my entire life. They had been in and out of hospitals, always wondering if my lungs were clear. I hated the attention, and I didn't want them fussing over me, so I tried to hide my asthma from them.

At seven, I wanted to fit in and enjoy the things that other kids did. I was embarrassed about the brown paper lunch sack that I brought to birthday parties because of my food allergies. I was sad and annoyed that I couldn't eat the pizza that all the other kids enjoyed. I felt like an outsider. I just wanted to be normal. Earlier in the day, I'd snuck a brownie containing walnuts at a swim team birthday party at our local YMCA. I didn't know it had nuts, but I did know that I wasn't allowed to eat it. I knew I shouldn't, but I did it anyway. A few minutes later my stomach hurt, and I ran to the bathroom. Unknowingly, I began to have a severe allergic reaction to the nuts. My older sister found me throwing up on the cold, wet ground of the locker room showers and ran to get help. My parents were called, and they rushed from home to pick me up.

They assumed I was having an asthma attack, because they didn't know about the brownie. The nebulizer treatment was worthless due to my throat swelling shut, and my parents witnessed me pass out as my airway became completely restricted. *I can't breathe...*

My mom had an uncanny ability to retain specific knowledge from her pre-med schooling and cautiously urged my dad in the car that day, "Dane, you have seven minutes to get her there before brain damage sets in." He got us there in four. Disregarding all rules, he drove on the shoulder, bobbing and weaving through cars down the two exits of the freeway to Scripps Children's Hospital.

My family ran inside, carrying my limp frame, and the nursing staff responded immediately. "STAT!" they shouted, which set in motion the medical process of trying to keep someone alive who is in anaphylactic shock. They intubated me to fill my lungs with oxygen. An IV administered the AAA rescue cocktail of adrenaline, antihistamines, and antacids to reverse the reaction. My parents watched, praying that I would wake up, hoping no brain damage had occurred.

I remember waking up to bright lights, beeping sounds, a sore throat, and many concerned faces hovering over me. My body was cold and shaky from the adrenaline, and I felt disoriented. I had no idea what had happened, but I knew I'd done something wrong. Shame follows "shoulds." I *should not* have eaten the brownie. I *should* have listened to my parents. I *should* be more obedient and a better daughter. I was filled with shame from all the shoulds in my thoughts.

I was born a quiet, independent, sneaky child. I didn't speak until I was three, because my very talkative and loving sister would speak for me. When I was young, I was often overlooked because I could sit silently and entertain myself for long periods of time. Thinking it was funny that no one noticed me, I would hide in the house and wait to see how long it took for someone to find me. Sometimes it was minutes, other times hours. Once, my family left the house for dinner without me, as I sat under the dining room table and watched them go. Secretly I wished they would notice me more. I felt invisible.

Much later in life, when I became a parent, I discovered that there is a chronic parental neurosis to keep a child alive, although no one ever shares this fun fact when you are considering having one. After my own flirtation with death, my parents had a legitimate and exponentially magnified reason to worry about my vitality. I'd wanted to be noticed more, and unfortunately, I got what I wanted.

My parents' extreme worrying didn't bode well for my teenage years. One night, I came home from a friend's house chewing mint gum, and my dad accused me of drinking peppermint schnapps. At thirteen, I became obsessed with Bob Marley. His slow, rocking rhythms and loving words soothed my anxious soul in the irrational and chaotic environment of my childhood.

My dad heard reggae music and screamed at me, "Are you smoking pot?!"

"No, Dad," I responded, confused, sheltered, and naive. "What's pot?"

"Don't play dumb—I know you are smoking pot! You can't listen to this anymore!" he bellowed like a bear and slammed the door.

"Asshole," I whispered under my breath as I locked the door and turned the music down. I would just have to listen to it with my headphones on.

After the nut incident, I was required by strict order from my dad to carry around an EpiPen and Benadryl in a hot pink fanny pack I called my "pink case." It was explained to me like this: I *should* always carry my pink case, so I wouldn't die. Shame follows shoulds.

My dad was driving my sister and me down a winding two-lane road one day, on the way to swim practice, when I realized I'd forgotten my pink case. Sitting in the back seat, terrified to tell him, I quietly spoke up.

"Daddy, I forgot my pink case."

"What'd you say?!"

"I forgot my pink case. I'm sorry, Daddy." I was so ashamed.

He grabbed the wheel and swerved the car, nearly hitting an oncoming van. I started to sob, "I'm sorry, Daddy. I didn't mean to. Please don't be mad."

"HOW COULD YOU FORGET IT, STACIANA!? YOU HAVE TO HAVE IT ALL THE TIME!" He raged as he made an illegal U-turn, foot to the floor, and sped back home to get it. I quietly cried as he continued to yell at me and my sister held my hand.

Every day of my childhood, from seven until I left the house for college, I held my breath. I shamefully hoped no one, especially my dad, would notice my wheezing or coughing. I held my breath when I was afraid. I held my breath when I made a mistake. I held my breath to hide my pain.

Learning to "breath-hold" became a skill I practiced in the water to strengthen my body and make an Olympic team. The trauma of holding back my breath and ultimately my voice kept me paralyzed from speaking up for myself. But my greatest strength grew from my greatest weakness: my breath.

# Under the Sea

*"[W]ater is a mirror for our darker emotions as much as it is an engine for our happiness. Water quiets all the noise, all the distractions, and connects you to your own thoughts."*

—Wallace J. Nichols, *Blue Mind*[7]

Nineteen eighty-eight was an impactful year for me. Not only did I unexpectedly flirt with death, I also watched the summer Olympics in Seoul, Korea, on television. I witnessed Janet Evans's gorgeous victory smile and windmill-stroke distance-freestyle swims that inspired little girls all over the world. She was young, only sixteen, but already a champion. Standing on the podium with arms in the air, beaming from ear to ear, she exuded the same vibrancy that I felt in the water. I knew after watching her that I wanted to swim in the Olympics too. I drew myself on the podium with a gold medal around my neck, just like Janet. I dreamed of being the best in the world. I had no idea about the reality of the process to become an Olympian, but I saw the end result of winning, and I wanted to be a champion too. I was seven.

My start in competitive swimming wasn't for glory. It began with a different, more pragmatic purpose: not for the hope of Olympic fame or fortune (profitable professional swimming was rare before Michael Phelps), but truly as an ingenious parental act to fulfill the desperate need for some quiet time.

My older sister, whom we called Lish, and I were very energetic little girls. At five and eight years old, we were constantly climbing the walls, literally up the doorframes, and jumping on the furniture to avoid the crocodiles and lava on the floor. We often had spontaneous dance parties on the coffee table, singing along with Cyndi Lauper and The Pointer Sisters. We loved dancing. If there was music on, Lish and I were dancing—and there was always music on in our house. We organized and performed fashion shows, pretending to be top models strutting down the runway, changing outfits until piles of clothes covered the floor. We kept our hardworking, tired educator parents entertained and annoyed. They decided the best thing for us, them, and the furniture was to sign us up for the swim team. The perfect babysitter.

Lish and I both struggled with asthma, and different doctors had suggested swimming would be the healthiest exercise for our lungs. It was known to strengthen lung capacity, and people spoke of the purity and humidity of the air directly above the water. Most importantly, Lish and I loved being in the water. We pretended to be mermaids, diving deep and exploring the bottom of the pool for hidden treasure, imagining swimming with the fish and discovering sunken ships. We knew every single word of the *Little Mermaid* soundtrack and sang along with it in the car daily. We imagined our legs turning into mermaid tails in the bathtub like Daryl Hannah in *Splash*.

During the first week of swim practice, we came home every night, quietly ate our entire dinner (including the tasteless boiled zucchini that Lish usually snuck to the bathroom and spit in the toilet), and fell asleep early. My parents were sold. We swam five days a week after school, and we were at the pool every weekend to play during open family swim. My best memories were underwater. My sister and I found pure joy and freedom in the clear blue water of our local pools. It was our happy place. Being underwater in a rainstorm, looking up at the surface as the raindrops rhythmically plunge below the surface, is magical. Everyone should experience it at least once.

I wasn't an athlete as a child, especially on dry land. Naturally uncoordinated on terra firma, I tripped over my own large feet, ran into walls, and often walked sideways into my friends. I was always picked last for team sports at school. I hated kickball, feeling humiliated when my classmates moved closer as I stepped up to the plate. But that all changed when I entered the water. With nothing to run into (besides the occasional end of the pool on backstroke), I gradually began to flourish. I chased my sister with an intrinsic motivation to be the best at an early age. And in the early stages of my swimming career, I wanted to go to practice every day so I would be allowed to jump off the high dive on Fun Fridays. I had no fear.

After years of staring at the black line on the bottom of the pool and racing anyone willing to accept my challenge (or secretly racing if they were unwilling), I started to improve my times and slowly gained some momentum. The beginning of my swimming career originated from the joy of being underwater. I have vivid, beautiful recurring dreams of being a sea creature, swimming under waves in the ocean. Maybe author Wallace J. Nichols understood those dreams when he quoted philosopher Alan Watts as saying, "You didn't come into this world. You came out of it, like a wave from the ocean. You are not a stranger here."[18]

I wondered if the catalyst for my swimming success, losing my hair to alopecia universalis when I was twelve, was an evolutionary change to return to my place of origin, the water.

# Fall to Pieces

## Fall 1993, Age 12

"I...(huh huh) fall...(huh huh)...to pieces..." I wailed, lying on the floor, singing along to Patsy Cline through gasping, body-shaking sobs. My concerned, empathetic dad stood outside the closed door of my bedroom, forehead against the doorframe, listening to me grieve, as tears filled his eyes.

An hour before, I had been mostly bald, with only small, patchy cascades of brown hair falling past my shoulders. I held on to the fragments of my past identity in denial of the current reality. I was a balding twelve-year-old girl.

"It doesn't look good, Stacer. Please let me shave it," my dad had pleaded.

"Okay," I conceded, trusting his opinion. He took his electric razor and carefully released the long, brown strands from my sensitive, aching skin. The physical pain radiated from my skull. Turmoil churned through my body. I held my breath, muscles tensed, and waited, debilitated by the fear of the inevitable.

When he finished, I ran to my bedroom for solitude. I had to look by myself. Intuitively I knew it wouldn't be easy. As I slowly shifted to center myself in front of the full-length mirror, I didn't recognize the person looking back at me. Watery eyes full of shock. Bald and afraid. *This isn't me*, I thought, standing alone, not even connected to my reflection. She had abandoned me in our implicit effort to be one. Taking in the separation between my perceived identity and the reality of my appearance, "How dare you?!" I accused her. And then I fell apart. Sinking to the floor, I melted into a ball of tears and rage. "I...(huh huh)...fall... (huh huh...) to pieces," I sang with Patsy. Her words helped me grieve. I knew she understood.

I hated my hair as a child. I hated brushing it. I hated washing it. I wanted nothing to do with it. Lish was in charge of brushing it in the mornings before school. As most eight-year-old big sisters would do to their five-year-old siblings, she ripped out knots with quick strokes of a brush as I cried in pain. My parents left early for work every morning, and they trusted her to get us both ready for school. We walked together to the bus stop in time to get picked up with the other neighborhood kids. I revered my sister. I followed her around like a puppy dog. She guided me through life. She still does. Reflecting on a different time in our world, I see we were very responsible, independent little girls.

I was a patient and obedient second-born child. These traits did *not* serve me well during a much different fatherly haircut from the past. When I was eight, my dad had decided to cut my hair. He was an amateur who worried about getting it perfectly even, a difficult challenge even for an experienced professional stylist. Straight hair shows every imperfection. I stood patiently on the linoleum kitchen floor with my knees locked as his untrained hands cut off five inches of hair, half an inch at a time.

After three and a half hours, I passed out. My dad caught me by my oversized white T-shirt as I fell backward, right before my head hit the floor.

"Stace, wake UP!" Lish shouted at me, laughing as I regained consciousness. "You passed out! Hahaha!"

I smiled back, happy I had made her laugh.

"Just a little bit longer, Stacer. I want to get it right," my dad reassured me as I stood up again.

"*Daaaaaad*, she just passed out! I think you're done." Lish always had my back and stood up to my dad often.

"Just a little bit longer..." he repeated quietly, reassuring himself.

God was preparing me through experience not to want my hair. Frankly, it's a pain in the ass. Time and money wasted to wash, cut, color, shave, wax...for what?

Becoming a teenager shifted my perspective about my hair, though. I realized the value of a cool hairstyle at school. Wanting to fit in with the other sixth-graders, I started to brush, wash, and style my hair daily.

In the fall of seventh grade, I stood in front of the bathroom mirror and brushed my long, brown hair to perfect the style of the popular girls in my class. I hoped if I looked like them, I would be popular too. The brush kept filling up with hair. Once, twice, three times, I cleaned it out. Yet it continued to collect clumps of hair with every brush stroke. I quickly filled the small bathroom trash can with hair. I felt no pain, just confusion.

*Am I dying? Do I have cancer?* Unaware that people with cancer lose their hair due to chemotherapy, not the disease, I felt certain I was very sick.

"MOM! I'm dying!!!" I ran to my mom, who was cooking in the kitchen, and showed her the contents of the trash can. She laughed at my dramatic preteen statement.

"Stace, you're not dying. You're a healthy kid," she reassured me. But the concern in her eyes as she looked at the trash can expressed a different message. "Let's go to the doctor to see what's going on."

After multiple doctors' visits with pediatricians, specialists, dermatologists, and allergists, I was told I had developed alopecia areata, an autoimmune disorder that causes inflammation that restricts the growth of the hair follicle until it falls out. The doctors explained that it could be stress-related or a genetic mutation.

One doctor in particular had the audacity to explain it to me like this: "We don't know if it'll fall out. We don't know *if* or *when* it'll come back. It may come back and then fall out again. We aren't certain why it happens, but it's suggested it may be caused by stress. But...you're fine. You're not dying." He paused, then asked, "Tell me, are you stressed?"

I was fucking livid! Who the fuck was "we," and why didn't "we" know anything?!

*Of course, I'm stressed, you asshole!* I thought. *My hair is falling out. I'm not fine! I can't go to school with a bald head!* I wish that at twelve I'd had the confidence to speak up to this doctor. Patronizing me with his authoritative and insensitive remarks, he was clearly detached from the emotional trauma of an adolescent girl losing her hair. I left his office feeling deflated.

Over the next three months, my hair loss progressed from alopecia areata (a few bald spots) to alopecia universalis, which caused total hair loss all over my body. Every day I would wake up and see my white pillowcase covered with brown hair. Clumps of long, wet hair stuck to the walls after every shower, as I literally and figuratively tried to wash my hands of the loss.

I was so scared and so sad, lying on the floor of my bedroom, grieving with Patsy.

My parents met with the middle school administrators, and I received special permission to wear hats. I hid under my hat for all of seventh grade. I didn't want to meet the eyes of the students and teachers staring. I pretended not to hear the cruel teasing that all middle school students engage in when the teachers aren't around. I became more introverted and had only a few close friends I could talk to about it.

My saving grace during this complete physical identity shift was swimming. I knew I didn't want to wear a wig. I imagined how awful it would be to swim in the pool one day and see my wig floating away. Also, I'd reached the age of noticing boys and fantasizing about having a boyfriend. In a split second, I envisioned how awful it would be to sit next to my made-up boyfriend and have to say, "Surprise! I'm bald!" That just seemed cruel and insincere for both of us. A wig wasn't for me.

My true friends were at the pool.

"I'm losing my hair," I explained to them. "I'm going to be completely bald. I'm not sure it is going to come back. But... it's not contagious," I smiled, trying to make light of the situation, hoping they would accept me.

"Cool!" they responded. "You're gonna swim faster!"

Their prophetic message lit a fire within me. In the water, I channeled all my anger and frustration from each shitty encounter I had with cruel middle school peers, inconsiderate doctors, and ignorant adults. I didn't need hair to swim. It felt incredible to dive into the pool and sense the cool water on the exposed nerve endings of my bald head. The pool formed my new identity. I was going to be a strong, successful swimmer. I was going to be a champion.

I felt liberated during the summer between seventh and eighth grade. I swam double practices, soaking up the sunshine four hours a day, and was free from hiding under a hat at school. I prayed every night for my hair to grow back, and amazingly enough, it started to grow. I was hopeful and carefree. *Back to normal*, I thought.

But at the beginning of eighth grade, the few inches of growth I'd achieved over the summer, making me look like a chia pet, began to fall out again. This time, my shock was replaced with anger. The doctor described a couple of options to grow my hair back: painful cortisone injections into my head and/or topical steroids that *might* help the hair grow.

"Unfortunately," he explained, "your body will adjust and become dependent on the medicine. You may grow back a full head of hair, but it's not guaranteed. And it will most likely fall out again if you stop using the medication." The uncertainty of these options drove me crazy. I didn't like the lack of control. I didn't want to be a slave to the medicine.

I couldn't pray, wait, and hope for my hair to grow back just to watch it all fall out again and again. I foresaw a torturous cycle, and I wanted to stop spinning from the fearful anticipation of loss. I didn't want to hide my condition, feeling terrified people might find out I was bald with every new encounter. I knew I had to embrace it in all aspects of my life. I wanted to consistently feel the liberation I felt at the pool, *if* I was brave enough to try. The only way to be free was to accept that I was bald, walk tall (which took me many years and experiences to accomplish), and move on. I had to go to school without a hat. I felt certain this was the choice I had to make to thrive.

"Mom, Dad, I think I need to go to school without a hat," I tentatively told my parents one night over dinner.

My mom was nervous for me. She worried I would be teased, and she was absolutely right. She worried people would stare, which they definitely did. Later, when I was in high school, she shared that she worried I wouldn't have a boyfriend. Luckily, God gave me the strength to get through difficult things, a strong knowledge of my own self-worth, and the courage to *be* my authentic self, no matter the cost.

I responded to my mom's fears with certainty: "Mom, if someone doesn't wanna be with me because I don't have hair, then they don't deserve to be with me," I stated firmly.

My mom smiled and apologized, "Of course. You're right, honey. I'm sorry."

This courage to be true to myself at thirteen didn't ease the pain of the first day of school without a hat. It was the hardest day of my emotional and social teenage life. I walked to school with my eyes down, thinking every swear word imaginable. *Shit. Fuck. Damn. Fuck. Shit. Shit. Fuck. Shit*, I repeated silently to myself. This mantra pushed me further down the path to freedom. One foot in front of the other, one powerful, inappropriate word with each step. As I walked through campus, I pretended not to hear the shouts, hollers, and laughter of middle school students

"Daaaaang! She's bald! Look at 'er!" They pointed and laughed. I kept walking.

It stung. It still does. But I knew it was worth the pain. I needed to break free from the chains that bound my spirit when I hid my condition.

I created a protective invisible bubble around me. I looked ahead to where I was walking, without focusing on anyone's face. This self-defense mechanism strengthened my resolve when navigating through crowds of strangers. I chose not to see their stares.

My mom admitted during this time of transition, "I have to walk next to you. I can't walk behind you, for fear of throat-punching all the people staring at you." (She didn't really say the throat-punching part, but I know she was thinking it. She grew up in Cleveland and is one tough lady.) Their stares made her angry. She wanted to protect me. But she couldn't. I had to learn to protect myself.

The blessing of alopecia is it weeds out the assholes. Now, I believe people when they show me how they act. And I choose to trust those who love me for *all* my qualities. How you behave and how you treat people is more important than what you look like. People who judge you only for your appearance will be surprised every time. I've learned to embrace the stares. I love making people look twice—once at my head, and once at my heart, as I walk with it open, lifted up, ready to accept love from deserving people, and ready to give it back.

# Another One Bites the Dust

## Spring 1996, Age 14

My sister and I had a love-hate relationship in high school. I loved her, and she hated me. At least that's how I felt most of the time. In 1999, I was a freshman and she was a senior. She struggled living in a house with preoccupied working parents, who were trying to deal with two hormonal teenage girls and two toddler boys at the same time. Absolute chaos: screaming, fighting, wrestling, crying, and tantrums from all of us. Lish needed her own space, but there was no space to be had in our small house. We shared everything.

On Christmas morning that year, our mom thought it would be funny to give Lish a toilet seat from Santa. She was tired of hearing my sister complain about having to share a bathroom with our brothers, who'd mastered the art of peeing all over the toilet and floor. As Lish unwrapped her present, hoping for something cool and exciting like car keys, shock overtook her face. Our mom grinned from ear to ear, proud of her prankster gift. "Now you can have your own seat to pee on," she said. "You don't have to share."

Our brothers, Curtis and Josef, impishly danced around flaunting their gifts and laughing at Lish, singing in unison, "You gotta toilet, you gotta toilet!"

Understandably, on more than one occasion, Lish locked the door to the bedroom that we shared, to create her own space free from siblings who didn't honor boundaries. One night, frustrated and in a full rage, our dad busted down the locked door to prove a point. Then he took the door completely off the hinges (probably because it was broken) and took it away to send her a message: "You will share. You will share your space, your clothes, your life." At the time, this threw her into full teenage tantrum mode, screaming, kicking, and yelling at our dad. I didn't understand her frantic frustration and need for space. I wasn't there yet developmentally or emotionally. We both thank the Lord we have each other now, but at the time it was difficult to see through the crowded environment to a future without all the chaos.

As her little sister, I wanted to wear her clothes, be friends with her friends, and do everything she did. I'd sneak into her closet when she wasn't home to try on her clothes and pretend I was her. The only thing we didn't share was a love for competition. At swim practice, I would get into her lane, insist on swimming behind her (she was still faster than me), and ride her wake, staying on her heels and touching her toes with every stroke as I tried to catch her and pass her. She put up with me. Our coach finally noticed her frustration and gave the seniors their own lane. I longingly watched her swim a few lanes away—and secretly raced her. She had every right to hate me. But she didn't.

Lish was my protector. She'd invite me to lunch with her friends to make sure I didn't have to eat by myself. They had senior privilege to drive off campus, and I felt so cool going with them as a freshman. She even brought me to her senior graduation party because she knew I wanted to go, despite the fact that it was only for seniors and I was not ready to be there socially. I sat in a corner and listened to Bob Marley, while she periodically checked on me. She had my back.

One day at club swim practice, our team was running on the side of the road for dryland training. Lish usually ran close to me to see if I was wheezing. She often reminded me to take my inhaler, because I tended to ignore my asthma and push myself through exercise. On this particular run, I tripped over a curb and skinned my knees. Another freshman boy on the team laughed and pointed at me, joking with his buddies. Lish saw the whole thing go down, ran over to the kid, and pushed him so hard it knocked him to the ground. "Punk!" she yelled, putting him in his place. He cowered at her size and strength. And he stopped making fun of me. I was in awe of her ability to protect me and not care about the consequences.

She and I had a blast on the high school swim team together. She loved the social aspect of high school swimming, and I loved the fact that we were going to *win* because we were on the team together.

Lish thrived in high school swimming because it was all about the team. She was naturally social and brought people together, making sure everyone had fun. There was less individual pressure because we had a team to swim for, not just ourselves. She was the team captain, deciding the color of our racing suits, organizing candy sales for a team fundraiser, and planning experiences for our team to bond over pre-meet dinners at Souplantation. We even created a behind-the-block dance to the beat of the song "Another One Bites the Dust" by Queen. As we stood behind the blocks preparing to race with our competitors, in the lanes next to us on either side, according to dual-meet protocol, the whole team would gather behind our lanes at the far end of the pool. They'd yell the chorus, "Doo, Doo, Doo, ANOTHER ONE BITES THE DUST!" We danced and pointed at the competition, smiling from ear to ear, confident in our ability to race and win with the help of our teammates' support. It was a blast.

ANOTHER ONE BITES THE DUST

In the spring of 1996, during the infancy of the internet and well before smartphones, information sharing was minimal. Coaches would call their results into the newspaper, and our dad would read the times of our local competitors to us each week. Our high school team, Carlsbad, had won every dual meet of the season leading up to our dual meet against our rival Torrey Pines. The athletes on the Torrey Pines High School swim team were cocky and entitled because they were league champions every year. Based on our success that season, we knew we had a shot at beating them. However, the Torrey Pines coaches intentionally did not submit their results and times to the local paper because they wanted to have an advantage when creating their lineup. Lish and I devised a plan to find out their times. The week before our dual meet against each other, Torrey Pines had a dual meet against San Pasqual High School. To figure out our best strategy to beat them, we wanted to see who swam which events and how fast. We asked our coach if we could go to the meet and scout their times instead of going to practice. Our coach thought it was a great idea, so a small group of us went.

In our small San Diego California Interscholastic Federation (CIF) bubble, our swim league, my sister and I were known as the Stitts Sisters. Plus, because of my bald head and our swimming reputation at the club level, we couldn't be anonymous if we tried. So the Torrey Pines coaches saw us discreetly recording times on the side of the pool with stop watches, and they got nervous.

The day of the Torrey Pines dual meet, we traveled to them on a yellow school bus, singing and laughing the whole way to the pool. They had the home pool advantage, but we had a fire in our bellies to win and a team that supported each other. We raced a strong competition that day, screaming behind the blocks of every teammate and encouraging them to score as many points as possible. It came down to the last relay, and they out touched us. Their pompous screams of victory hurt a little more in that moment. However, in an amazing turn of events, our scouting mission the week before had put doubt in their minds. They made the mistake of not trusting their own ability to win and gave in to the fear of possible defeat. The Torrey Pines coaches had made a last-minute decision to enter an ineligible swimmer to guarantee the win. We found out after the last race, and our team ended up winning the dual meet. Their team was disqualified for cheating. We'd intimidated them without even trying.

After the swim meet, we all got on the yellow school bus to go home. Our coach, Mr. Walker, walked down the aisle of the bus and handed each teammate a yellow rose. He hadn't expected us to win and wanted to give us something to remember the moment and cheer us up. His nickname was Chip because we all joked that he was formerly a Chippendales dancer. He had a fireman's physique, including the mustache, which sat between a beautiful smile and kind eyes. His laid-back attitude and good looks made all the high school girls twitterpated with boy-crazy hormones. The fact that he was giving each one of us a rose was more than some girls could handle, and they giggled with awkward teenage silliness. When he got to my sister and me, his grin widened, knowing our actions had helped to secure the win. "Thank you, ladies," he said. He nodded and kept walking. We had no idea the repercussions of our actions would work so well in our favor. We beat Torrey Pines. We were now league champions. The feeling of victory was sweet, especially sharing it with my sister.

# San Diego CIF

## May 1996, Age 14

It's difficult to share a podium. After our high school team won the league championship, my sister and I went on to compete individually at CIF in San Diego. This year was the year that Lish had a chance to finally win her event, the 100-meter breaststroke. She had been close to winning over the previous three years but hadn't achieved it yet. The past champion had graduated, and now was her moment to shine. As a senior, she could finally be a CIF champion. The only problem was that her best event was also *my* best event. If Lish had her way, I think she would have liked to share the podium with me. But manifesting a tie down to 1/100th of a second on an electronic timing system is difficult and rare. (Anthony Ervin and Gary Hall Jr. did it in the 50-meter freestyle in the 2000 Olympics in Sydney, and we were all amazed.) And if I had my way, I was going to win—even if it meant thwarting her final chance at glory. That "take no prisoners" attitude is what pushed me to become an

Olympic champion, but it didn't bode well for a copacetic relationship with my sister during the week leading up to CIF.

That week was tense in the house. My parents didn't know how to navigate the situation between us. My times had been getting closer and closer to Lisha's times during the dual-meet season, and the potential for one of us to win was high. But who would it be? They knew I was only looking at the win and not considering her feelings. And they knew my sister needed more space. She lacked the confidence in her own ability to win and had to put up with her little sister chasing her down like a rabbit in a horse race. She couldn't protect me in this situation, and she didn't need to. She needed to protect herself from me, putting her needs first before mine, and she had not done that before.

The morning of the race was chilly. Excitement filled the air as the swimmers prepared, stretching on the deck in their parkas and warming up in the pool. The parents set blankets out on the wet metal bleachers, claiming their territory to watch their children compete. The morning sunbeams illuminated the steam as it rose up from the pool, the warm water evaporating into the cool morning air. The steam was so thick, it allowed for my sister to be covert, happily hidden from sight.

She avoided me because she needed space, and I took the hint.

We did our own warm-ups separate from each other. I did my pre-race routine; she did hers. She hung out with her friends, trying to stay relaxed; I hung out by myself, listening to music. Our parents sat in the stands, huddled next to each other, and watched the careful dance in anticipation.

Behind the blocks before the race, time stopped. My sister and I stood there, waiting for the official to blow the whistle to invite us up onto the blocks. Out of habit I wanted to do the "Another One Bites the Dust" dance we had made up together, but in this instance, it didn't feel appropriate. She was my idol, my teammate, my sister, and my friend. I wanted to be her, and in order to do that, I would have to beat her. There could only be one champion. The stands were silent as we stood on the blocks, tense and prepared to swim the best and most difficult race of our lives. My parents held their breath. No matter the result, the outcome wasn't going to be easy to deal with at home. One of us was going to lose.

We swam four lengths of the race stroke for stroke, fighting next to each other for the same thing. We turned on each wall together, pushing each other to be better. My legs burned on the last twenty-five meters, and I heard the crowd cheering to the rhythm of our strokes. When we finished with a synchronous stroke into the wall, I had no idea who'd won. I looked up at the clock and saw our times. I had touched her out!

I felt so much joy and was elated—until the moment I looked over at my sister. I wanted her approval, affirmation that I had done well. But she was upset. Head in the gutter, disappointment shook her body with each sob as she cried from the overwhelming stress of the day and the pain of losing the race she was supposed to win. I felt her sadness, and my joy from selfish victory disappeared. I should have let her win. I should have thought of her needs in that moment. I had many more chances to feel the glory days of high school swimming, but she did not. It would have made a difference to her if she had won. She should have won. Shoulds lead to shame.

She got out of the pool, teary-eyed as they announced her name and handed her a silver medal: "Alisha Stitts, second place!" She waited there as they announced my name: "And in first place, Staciana Stitts!" The parents clapped as I got out of the pool and received my medal. But instead of waving in celebration, I stared at the ground, tail tucked between my legs. I couldn't look at Lish or anyone else, ashamed of my actions. She grabbed me and hugged me. The great space that had been between us all week was finally bridged. Holding her, I cried and said, "I'm sorry Lish. I'm so sorry I beat you."

"Oh, shut up, Stace! You're not sorry, and I'm so proud of you." She laughed through tears. She squeezed me tighter as we cried together. "Congratulations." Her unconditional selfless love for me was greater than her own selfish ambition. She embodied God's love and grace. And I was filled up, knowing that the person I revered the most was proud of me.

# Trash Bag

## October 1998, Age 17

I stood on the ten-meter platform with my plum-painted flower toenails curled over the hard, thick cement edge, as I looked down at my fear. People slowly trickled out of the college football game and started to form a crowd outside, observing my hesitation through the floor-to-ceiling glass windows that framed the University of Iowa aquatics center. Feeling the need to encourage or taunt me, they began to bang on the glass in unison, joyously chanting, "Jump, jump, jump, jump!" with the swimmers below. The noise reverberated through the dark, indoor aquatics facility and competed with the sound of my pounding heart. As I watched more people outside curiously drawn to the action, my stomach turned and my ego urged me, *You better do it now, or the pressure will only get worse.*

Just a few minutes prior, I'd been swimming laps with the college swim team during my recruiting trip to the

University of Iowa. The girls on the team had explained the rite of passage that all incoming freshmen had to do when they came to compete for the varsity swim team: jump from the ten-meter diving platform during initiation week.

"Do you want to jump off the ten-meter?" the team asked a few of us recruits.

"Yes!" I answered quickly with a huge smile on my face.

They smiled back at me and encouraged the others who were more reluctant. "If you decide to come here, you will have to do it, so you might as well do it now."

"I'm in," I repeated.

I was born to live from a place of "yes." Every part of my being is an optimist, including my relationship with fear. Once, when I was younger, my dad said to me, "I'm more worried about you than your sister because you aren't afraid of anything." I was proud of this statement even before I could process why he felt this way. But he was wrong. I *was* afraid of things. I just never let the fear stop me.

And now I found myself once again leaning into the discomfort, pushing past the idea that I couldn't do something because I was scared.

"Shit," I quietly said to myself. I held my breath—and jumped.

Time slowed down as I fell toward the water. Three seconds of gravity's force felt like an eternity. I was out of control and afraid. My pointed toes broke the surface, and my outstretched T-shaped arms smacked the water with a tingling sensation that ran from my fingertips to my armpits. I stayed suspended underwater for a moment, in the place that brought me the most comfort, to recover from the fiery sting awakening all of my sensory receptors. As my head broke the surface to come up for air, I heard the crowd cheering and the girls laughing around me. I had conquered my fear again. And my confidence grew with each small victory.

My junior year in high school, I was the top recruit in the United States for the 100 breaststroke. I had the privilege of taking fully paid recruiting trips to five colleges of my choice. Lish was a sophomore in college at the University of Iowa, and I missed her dearly. She had gone there on a swimming scholarship, and I wanted to check out the school and have a fun weekend with her.

My sister was always the beautiful, confident one in our sibling dynamic. She was hyperaware of fashion and makeup, and she could put any outfit together and look fabulous. I was shy and antisocial, and I only understood fashion with her guidance. I never felt pretty compared to her, and losing my hair magnified this feeling immensely when I was in high school. I had confidence in my body as an athlete but not in my appearance.

After the diving experience at Iowa, the swim team took the recruits to a dance club later that night. As we walked into the club, I hesitated. I still wasn't comfortable being bald in new public places. Lish looked at me—really looked at me—and saw my fear. She grabbed my hand and pulled me to the side of the doorway. The lights flashed and the music blared, calling us to come in.

"Stace, you love to dance, right?" She knew the answer based on our many years of dance parties together on our parents' coffee table.

"Yes." I looked down, hunched over in worry about the inevitable stares.

"So, here's the deal: I could wear a trash bag and walk into this club with my shoulders back, my head held high, an open heart, and a smile on my face, and people would notice me."

"Yeah, I know. You're beautiful," I agreed with her.

"No, no, you don't get it. What I'm saying is, YOU could wear a trash bag and walk into this club with your shoulders back, your head held high, an open heart, and smile on your face, and people would notice you. Anyone can. It doesn't matter what you look like or what you're wearing for people to think you're beautiful. People will want to talk to you based on how you walk into a room. That's confidence, and it's what makes someone gorgeous." My sister is fucking awesome.

I watched her walk into the club exactly as she said: head up, shoulders back, open heart, smile on her face, like she owned the place. It was magnetic. *She* was magnetic. And I followed her every move. I was amazed by how it made me feel. We danced all night and I felt so much joy.

Her words and actions made a lasting impact on me. She was right; people notice someone's energy. When you walk into a room scared or nervous, people feel it and wonder what's wrong. But when you walk into a room radiating joy and love, people feel it and want to be near you. That's attraction. That's connection. I practice this daily, and it has helped me to receive love from many different people, strangers and friends alike.

# PART 2: FIRE

*"What hurts you, blesses you. Darkness is your candle."*

—Rumi[19]

# Belief

## Summer 1997, Age 15

"*Staciana!* What are you doing?! That's not breaststroke!! Get out! Just get out!" The early morning sunlight reflected through the steam that rose off the clear blue water's surface of the Irvine Heritage Park Aquatics Complex, where we trained for summer practices.

I knew my new coach meant well. I wasn't afraid of him, because he yelled at me with a smile on his face. But I also knew he was serious. What I was doing didn't constitute an efficient "best-in-the-world breaststroke." This coach, Dave Salo, was vibrant, confident, and passionate about fast, efficient swimming.

Four weeks earlier, my parents had driven me up to Irvine to watch a swim practice and explore the opportunity to train with Irvine Novaquatics (NOVA). I'd qualified for senior nationals the spring of my sophomore year in high school at age fifteen, with pure hard work and spastic grit, training with a small club team in San Diego. Nationals were long-course competitions, meaning they were always held in a fifty-meter pool. I had never trained in a long-course pool. One year earlier, my family had watched the 1996 Olympics, and my dad told me that Amanda Beard was training with NOVA only sixty miles from our house. We were the same age and swam the same event, and she had achieved what I wanted: Olympic glory! Of course I wanted to train with her.

Sitting on the cement grandstands and observing the swim practice that first afternoon in late spring, I was amazed by the sound of the water. "Dad, can you hear that? The water sounds different." The swimmers practiced at a level of intensity and technique that created a deep, resonating vibration. I'd never heard water move with such power and force before. And then Dave walked in. "He stands balanced on both feet," my dad remarked. "That's gotta be him."

Dave exuded confidence, knowledge, and absolute dominance over his space. The bold alpha energy radiated from him as he paced the deck, like a lion ruling his kingdom, observing and technically critiquing the large group of swimmers. His sets were detailed and intentionally complex, to keep the swimmers engaged and entertained as they trained.

After the practice, my parents and I walked down to the deck to speak with him. My heart raced with excitement and my stomach fluttered with anxiousness.

"Hey there! I'm Dave." He shook my hand with such strength and had a genuine smile on his face.

"I'm Staciana. It's nice to meet you."

"What can I do for you?"

"Well, I'm looking for long-course pool time because I qualified for senior nationals, but I don't have a fifty-meter pool to train in."

"Okay, what are your goals for swimming?"

I looked him straight in the eye and said with confidence, "I want to be the best in the world. I want to make the Olympic team."

I waited in the brief silence, anticipating the usual anxious, dismissive laugh that comes from adult insecurity and pessimism. But instead of being intimidated by my intense stare, he leaned into it.

"Well, we break world records all the time in practice," he confidently responded while staring intently back at me. My eyes grew wide.

He laughed at my surprise, shrugged his shoulders, and threw his hands out, adding, "The swimmers have *fins* on... but they practice swimming *fast* every day. They know what it feels like to break world records."

I was hooked. I wanted to be there. I felt it in my bones. His belief in himself as a coach and his swimmers' ultimate potential would help me achieve my dreams. And my parents agreed.

Four weeks later, Dave was frustrated watching my uncoordinated stroke and yelled at me to get out of the water. I thought he was kicking me out. But he had other ideas. He threw two kickboards on the ground a few feet apart.

"Lie down!" He demanded. "I want you to place your elbows on that board," he said, pointing to the top board, "and your knees on this one." I obediently lay on my belly, placing my joints on the kickboards. "Now, I want you to lift your belly off the ground and pull your belly button into your spine like you are trying to go over a barrel. Only your elbows and knees should be touching the ground. Kick your feet up to your hips like you were going to do a breaststroke kick and hold them there."

*What the heck?* I wondered. Not only was it difficult to do and painful on my bones, it also felt extremely awkward and unnatural. I had never been in this position before.

"Now you are going to hold that position for two minutes. THIS is breaststroke. I have no idea what you are doing in the water, but it's not this." He laughed and walked away.

His methods were unorthodox. But they were effective. I trusted him and worked hard to make the technique changes he suggested daily. He recognized that verbal instruction didn't work for me. I needed to feel it. And this was how I could learn it, by practicing the correct position on land, which produced the muscle memory to repeat it in the weightless and seemingly ever-changing space and resistance of water. Gravity on land was a different feedback mechanism than in water. When swimming, I had little to no body awareness in space because I didn't have to know where my body was. The water embraced me no matter what shape I took on. Somehow this dryland exercise made sense for my brain.

I trained with NOVA for six weeks that summer—five hours a day, six days a week—to prepare for nationals and junior nationals with the team at the beginning of August. Two weeks into training, my body folded with fatigue as I got into the car after practice and said to my mom through tears, "I don't know if I can do this. It's so hard, and I'm so scared. Today we had to do this hypoxic training in the little pool. It was so crowded. Dave had half the group of forty kids on one side and half the group on the other. One side would sprint swim in one direction on the surface and the other side would kick underwater underneath them going the other direction. You couldn't come up for a breath, or you would run into a swimmer. I was panicked and petrified."

Self-preservation is strong in humans, and the fear of death creates feelings of desperation. I didn't want to let Dave down—I was so eager to please—but I wasn't sure I was capable of what he demanded of us physically and mentally.

My mom reassured me, "Stace, you can do this. You're just exhausted. It'll get easier. Just give it a little more time. It's hard to learn new things. Remember why you wanted this in the first place."

I flashed on the image of myself on the Olympic podium, smiling like Janet Evans. *Yes, I can do it*, I thought. I just had to remember my why.

Nationals that summer were held in Nashville, Tennessee. I traveled by myself for the first time, because my parents couldn't afford to go with me. When I arrived for my event, I was starstruck. Jenny Thompson was stretching in the corner, preparing for her race. I had watched her on TV at the 1996 Atlanta Olympics and couldn't believe we were on the same pool deck. Dave saw how nervous I was after the warm-up, so before my race he told me, "I want you to go into the warm-up pool and do flips underwater and play."

"What do you mean?" I looked at the small five-lane, twenty-five-yard, three-foot-deep warm-up pool and thought, *The veterans in there will kill me if I'm doing somersaults on the bottom of the pool in their way.*

He had never said anything like that to me in the six weeks of "proper technique guidance."

"It'll help you. Just do it. You belong here. You've trained hard. Now it's time to have some fun and celebrate." He reassured the nervous "impostor" identity that was creeping into my psyche. "You have nothing to lose. This is just for experience."

Something clicked within me. I heard my dad's voice inside my head: *Just dance, Stace.*

As I flipped in the warm-up pool underwater, I felt the joy of swimming with my sister, dancing like mermaids. The release of tension and expectations opened up the space for relaxed performance. Dave was right; my body knew what to do. It was my brain that needed to get out of the way. I danced through the water with ease during my race, letting my body take over and my mind relax. I dropped four seconds in my 100 breaststroke. Dave looked at me after the race with a light in his eyes and said, "Junior nationals next week will be fun!"

The next week at junior nationals in Clovis, NOVA brought an army of high school elite swimmers. Twenty-five of us filled three fifteen-passenger vans and made the four-hour trek to what we snarky teenagers called the "armpit of California." It was 110 degrees all day, and we all brought misters to stay cool.

My only prior experience at junior nationals was with my sister for our swim club in San Diego, and I was disqualified (aka "DQ'd") twice due to nervousness. Once, my leg wouldn't stop shaking, and the official called me as a false start due to too much movement on the block before the signal to go. The second time, I took two kicks into the wall without a stroke in between, which was something I hadn't done since I was a six-year-old novice swimmer. I was ashamed and mortified by my performances. Nervous energy is the ultimate saboteur if not channeled appropriately.

The morning of the 200 breaststroke in Clovis, I tentatively walked to Dave on the side of the pool before my race. I stared at the pen stuck into the collar of his white polo shirt. He asked me in our routine pre-swim check, "What's your race strategy?

"Not to get DQ'd," I laughed.

"Okay, well, that's a start." He dismissed my nerves and low expectations of myself. "Remember your training. I think it's gonna be a good race for you."

I swam my best time, relaxed and free, and made it back to finals top seed.

As I walked up to Dave after the race, he grinned and said, "Now you get to pick your walk-up song!" His mouth gaped open wide with a smile, as he eagerly awaited my joyful response, knowing how much I loved music.

"Really?!" I jumped up and down, pumped about the surprise.

That evening before my race was the same routine, but this time with a different message from Dave. "I think you can win this," he said. He was standing on both feet. And that's all I needed.

I walked out tall and proud with a smile on my face, dancing to the escalating tone and the driving electronic beat of "Firestarter" by Prodigy. The flame in my belly had smoldered for so long, suppressed by lack of belief and the wrong types of fuel. The feelings of anger, rage, and rebellion that I'd used to train weren't enough to make it grow. But now, I was filled with the courage of a coach's belief in me and the joy of racing to win. The fire within me danced to the music, burning bright, and then surged, warming me up. I had become a fire-breathing dragon with each deep breath of focus, determination, and faith. I won junior nationals through the power of belief and the freedom to dance.

# Trials

## August 11, 2000, Age 18

"So, how *do* you pronounce your name?" The six-foot brunette opponent towered over me in the ready room with a huge shit-eating grin on her face, and I felt like she was fucking with me. "Because I've heard all different pronunciations."

I responded by growing an inch taller (thanks to an accessible posture change I had learned in yoga) and said through a powerful smile, like I was announcing myself to the world, "Staciana Stitts." Her intimidation tactics would not extinguish my fire. In fact, they fueled it. I immediately felt superior, taking back the power she wanted to have over me.

*I'm gonna kick her ASS!* I thought.

We have no idea the impact our words make on others. They can be powerful—and easily misunderstood. Each individual interprets words and attaches meaning to them based on their own experience and the lens through which they see the world.

It was the night of the finals of the 100 breaststroke at the 2000 United States Olympic Trials in IUPUI Natatorium in Indianapolis. I had trained for three years with *this* specific race in mind. As Malcolm Gladwell suggested in his book *Outliers*, I had already trained over ten thousand hours for this exact moment.

Three nights before, when our team of twenty-five NOVA athletes had arrived in Indiana, we went to a famous steakhouse called the Loon Lake Lodge for dinner. I made the mistake of eating a bite of my teammate's elk that I *"had to try"* according to him, because it was so delicious. I didn't expect meat to have nuts on it, nor did I think about the possible contamination of the sauce smothered all over it.

My tongue started to itch and swell, and I knew I was in trouble.

"Dave," I said, having quickly walked over to the booth where he and the other coaches were talking. "I ate a nut and need to get to the hospital as soon as possible."

"Okay, let's go." He sensed the urgency of the situation and did not hesitate.

I slipped into the back of the passenger van and pulled the EpiPen out of my swim bag.

"What are you doing back there?" Dave inquired.

"I gotta give myself an EpiPen in my leg. Don't look. Just drive," I said, with my pants halfway down, shaking with fear and adrenaline.

The restaurant sat at the corner of a large intersection in Indianapolis. Across the street was our hotel, and luckily—or, as I like to think of it, *a blessing from above*—the hospital was on the third corner.

Familiar with the situation, I had Dave drop me off at the emergency room and told him to meet me inside so he could park the van. "STAT," I said to the intake nurse as I approached the desk. "I ate a nut, going into anaphylaxis. Need help." I barely got the words out through short, adrenaline-filled statements. I could feel the shaking start as the epinephrine made the blood rush from my extremities to my core.

The hospital staff rushed me back, hooked me up to an IV, and placed a heart-rate monitor and pulse oximeter on my thumb. The past experiences of anaphylaxis, filled with fear and trauma, came rushing back to me. I thought Dave was going to be mad at me, like my dad had been in the past.

When Dave walked into the room, it felt like all my dreams were falling apart. "I'm so sorry," I sobbed apologetically through tears of grief and fear. I felt like I had screwed everything up and thrown it all away. Then I panicked, "You can't give me anything!" I pleaded to the nurses. "I could test positive when they drug test me!" If I tested positive after my races, I would be disqualified from going to the Olympics.

"Staciana, don't be silly," Dave laughed at my singularly focused mindset. He had a calm confidence that made him such a great coach. "You can't make the Olympic team if you're dead." His logic made sense, but I was still apprehensive. He reassured me, "We'll get the doctors to write a note about what happened. I'm sure it'll be fine. Let's just get you better first."

"Dave, you can*not* tell my parents what happened. If they know I ate a nut tonight, they will have doubts in their head that I can make the team and I need EVERYONE to believe." I was superstitious and understood the power of a collective belief in something.

"Staciana, you're on the right path. Think how the restaurant, the hotel, and the hospital were all together on the same intersection, forming a triangle. That's not a coincidence." He knew I was superstitious and played that card to influence me in a positive way. He also knew if the hospital had been farther away, he might not have been having the same conversation with me—or any conversation at all.

"Promise me you and the other coaches won't say anything to my parents."

"I promise."

Two days later, mostly recovered from the incident, I swam in the prelims of the 100 breaststroke. The night before, I'd put on my racing suit and danced in front of a mirror to shake off the nerves. I was excited and anxious to get the first swim out of the way. I'd consistently been top five in the country for the last two years, and I knew I was capable of making it back to the trials' top sixteen.

And I did.

I swam a 1:08.78 in prelims, going under 1:09 for the first time, and gained confidence knowing I made it back fourth into the semifinals that night. I was seated next to Kristy Kowal, and she was projected, with Megan Quann, to make the team in the event. They were the favorites. I loved being the underdog. No pressure, plus a feeling of rebellion if I did what I came to do. *Fuck 'em*, I always thought when the implied narrative was that I wouldn't make it. *I'll show you.*

I made the Olympic team because of belief. Yes, there was a LOT of hard work through years of training and sacrifice to prepare. But everyone at that level trains hard in their own way. Everyone is in peak physical shape. The ones who believe are usually the ones who make the team. It's that extra little bit of mental strength and collective spirit that pushes you beyond what you think you can do.

My dad videotaped the semifinals race sitting in the photographer media section. (His high school rule-breaking spirit lived on in moments of perceived necessity.) I always swam with my eyes closed because blocking out the visual stimulus helped me tap into something deeper. I could get into a state of flow, muscles doing what they needed in a rhythmic, closed-looped motor skill[20] (in which repetitive motion becomes reflexive and decisions are unnecessary), to swim with speed and grace—although that didn't mean I always swam in a straight line.

I gave it my best effort in the semifinals for seventy meters, and then something inside of me shut down. My muscles were still moving, neurons still firing, but my heart had stopped giving 100 percent, with thirty meters to go.

I swam a 1:08.02, finishing second to Kristy, who went a 1:07.96. I couldn't believe the race was so close. I'd assumed she'd made her move in the last thirty meters. But watching the video back, she hadn't. I knew at that moment that I had her. "I can beat her," I said, looking at my dad, eyes shining, with a huge grin of joy on my face. I knew I had more in me, and I couldn't wait to swim again.

"Oh my goodness, where did you get that?!" I asked a coach I knew who was passing by me while eating an ice cream sandwich the next night. I had my headphones on, along with my sparkly black flared yoga pants and my team NOVA T-shirt over a long-sleeved shirt with a tiger on the front, which my sister had given me to embody the spirit of the dominant predator. I methodically and reflexively performed my stretching routine in a meditative dance to prepare for my finals race.

The coach said, "I got it from the coaches' hospitality." I imagined the magical room of unlimited free food that was off-limits to the hungry swimmers.

"Can you get me one?" I smiled with a hopeful plea.

"Sure!"

Nervous about sabotaging my race, I only ate half of the delicious treat. I knew I should intuitively listen to my cravings, but also in moderation.

While I was eating the sandwich, Eric Wunderlich, an Olympic breaststroker from the 1996 Atlanta Games, came up to me and gave me a pep talk. "I wanted to tell you: I've been to three trials," he said. "I've gotten everything from eighty-third place, two third places, and a second. I made the mistake of watching everyone else. When I marched out, I was worried about where people were in the stands, who I was next to in the pool, etc. I wasn't focusing on what I needed to do. Just do your own thing and you'll do great."

His words of wisdom filled me with a boost of confidence. He chose to give advice to *me*. He believed in me. I was grateful for the joy that came from his selfless action to connect and strengthen my belief.

Before the finals race, Dave also guided me with carefully chosen words: "Just swim your own race. Keep driving forward, finish hard into the wall, and relish the moment for a while. Don't even look up at the time for a moment. Just cherish the fact that you gave it your all and did your best." He took off all the pressure to place first or second that everyone feels overwhelmed by at trials. "Before you turn around, I want you to take the time to close your eyes and ask yourself, 'Did I do everything possible to swim my best race?' If the answer is 'yes,' I want you to be happy, regardless of the place number by your name."

I swam the race with my eyes closed. At thirty-five meters into the race, I felt my hand hit the lane line. I opened my eyes for a split second, and thought, *Dammit Stace, get in the middle of the lane. Swim straight!*

My college teammate and friend Anthony Ervin was at the far end of the fifty-meter pool, cheering for me as I swam toward him, and he yelled what I was thinking: "Gooooo Stace! Goooooo Stace! NO! Go *straight*, Stace!!!"

The father of positive psychology, Martin E.P. Seligman, describes a state of flow, or engagement, in the original theory of Authentic Happiness:

> The second element [of Authentic Happiness], engagement, is about flow: being one with the music, time stopping, and the loss of self-consciousness during an absorbing activity...if you ask people who are in the flow what they are thinking, they usually say, "nothing."...There are no shortcuts to flow. On the contrary, you need to deploy your highest strengths and talents to meet the world in flow.[21]

For most of this race, I was in the flow, employing my highest strengths in the moment. However, thirty meters from the finish, it started to hurt, and I was gaining consciousness of the pain. Slowly slipping out of the flow state, I became aware of the familiar muscular fatigue that hit me at the end of each race from full exertion. I gritted my teeth, kept driving forward, and thought, *You CANNOT give up on this one. THIS IS IT! There isn't another chance. You have to finish THIS one!* I tapped into the energy of the stands cheering. I watched myself from above, joining the crowd's consciousness, and knew I had to keep driving forward. Dancing with the rhythm of my breath, I could feel the energy surging me onward like a wave. All my thoughts stopped, and the force beyond language pulled me to the wall.

I made the team, out-touching Kristy by 1/100$^{th}$ of a second, the smallest margin possible. I swam a 1:07.79 for second place (the only time second feels like first) behind Megan Quann. Kristy was third with a 1:07.80.

And the whirlwind of chaos and emotion was released. I broke down in tears from the relief. The weight of every decision I had made for the last three years fell off my shoulders. All the sacrifices had been worth it. I was an Olympian. Forever.

The defining moment lasted for eternity. My teammates surrounded me, crying and hugging me. Dave was hysterical behind my lane. Crying tears of joy, he kept pointing at the scoreboard, which showed a "2" by my name, yelling, "It's a two! It's a two!" For good luck, he had worn the sweater vest I'd given him for his fortieth birthday, and it made me smile knowing I had brought him so much joy.

We achieve more together than alone. I could not have made the Olympic team without Dave's belief, without my team's support, without my family's sacrifices. And that shared connection and collaboration to achieve greatness also brings a shared sense of emotion. This energetic emotion connects us, flows among us, and surrounds us. The shared experience and shared consciousness define our humanity.

# Disillusioned

The Olympics were a place of romanticized dreams, filled with darkness and light entwined together by many shades of gray. The night I qualified for the team, I had no idea where the whirlwind of chaos was going to take me. I could never have imagined the darkness in the depths I would have to swim through. The pressure of the depths consumed me, and I felt like I was drowning.

## August 11, 2000, Age 18

Kristy sat at the edge of the warm-down pool, legs hanging over the edge into the water. She held a bottle of water in her hand, cap still on, untouched. Her shoulders rounded forward, protecting her heart, and her eyes looked down into the deep abyss of the diving well. She exuded disappointment and shame.

It had been twenty minutes since the finals of the 100 breaststroke at the Olympic Trials in 2000. I sat down next to her, copying her posture, gave her a huge hug, and admitted, "I'm sorry." I wasn't sorry for out-touching Kristy, but I felt terrible for making her feel this way. I felt her pain and wanted to lessen it.

"Don't be sorry. I've been here before," she said, referring to her third-place finish at trials four years earlier, in 1996.

"Just go for it in the 200. You're so strong in that race," I suggested. Kristy had won NCAAs many times and was the fastest in the country in the 200 breaststroke. Her tall frame and long, lean strength were unmatchable at the longer distance.

"I know. Thank you," she remarked.

All the competitive hate I had felt toward her in the ready room before the race vanished as soon as I felt her pain. I'd hurt her, and I hurt *with* her. We were connected, one and the same. It could have easily been me sitting there.

Three days later, I watched Kristy make the Olympic team in the 200 breaststroke and felt immense joy with her. I also felt overwhelming relief that my actions hadn't prevented her from achieving her dreams. I gave her a huge congratulatory hug. We were teammates now, possibly friends? I hoped this was true...but things got complicated when we arrived at the Olympic training camp in Pasadena.

## August 22, 2000, Age 18

One morning in practice at camp, the people who had qualified for the 100s of strokes were practicing relay starts, and Kristy was practicing with us. Confusion set in. *What's she doing?* I ignorantly thought. *She didn't qualify in the 100 breast.* The dark, daunting clouds of premonition crept into my thoughts. People say ignorance is bliss. I had no idea the paradigm shift I was about to experience. As hard as my childhood was, I was born an optimist and fairly sheltered from the shades of gray that were coming. I thought things were black and white. I had a strong moral code of right and wrong and believed in fairness. But the shadow cast over this view was too big for me to remain in the light of ignorance.

The International Olympic Committee (IOC) and the United States Olympic Committee (USOC) had a financial incentive program in place for coaches and athletes for the Olympics. The personal coaches received medal money if their swimmer placed in the top three at the Olympics, including relays. The swimmers received money as well if they were done with their NCAA eligibility. I was still considered an amateur because I was swimming for UC Berkeley at the time and was not allowed to take the medal money. This amateur status blinded me to the dark actions driven by greed.

Kristy's coach, like all the other coaches except mine, was pushing for her to be on the 400 medley relay due to her newly professional status, having just finished her eligibility for the NCAA. Historically, the U.S. relays had won more often than not at the Olympics, so placement on the relay was crucial for her financial gain—and a bonus for him.

Later that afternoon, back at the hotel, I asked my roommate what was going on. Her past experience from the 1996 Olympics made her wise about the politics of USA swimming. "Your relay spot is not guaranteed. It's up to the discretion of the coaching staff who they choose to put on those relays."

"Really?" I was shocked.

"Really. You should go talk to Richard and tell him you really wanna be on that relay."

"You think?"

"Yes, definitely," she said.

"Okay."

Richard Quick was intimidating. He was a highly successful coach from Stanford and had been the head Olympic coach for five Olympics in a row: 1984, 1988, 1992, 1996, and 2000. Later, he coached his sixth in 2004. He was considered swimming royalty, and I had to go talk to him.

My anxiety was heightened by the fact that I had turned him down the year prior when he was recruiting me to attend Stanford. I told him I didn't want to come on a visit because I knew I wanted to attend Cal.

"No one turns down Stanford!" he incredulously bellowed through the phone.

His entitlement and anger confirmed it wasn't the place for me, and I was grateful I had the courage to hang up the phone with the hope of never having to talk to him again. Man, was I wrong. Now I had to confront him. It shouldn't have felt like a favor, but the power struggle between coach and swimmer is complicated and challenging to navigate when you're young. I assumed he would remember my rejection and choose Kristy over me for the relay. It was my turn to feel the sting of rejection.

I knocked on his hotel room door that evening, hoping to speak with him, and he answered the door wearing only his boxers. "Hello, Staciana," he said with a Cheshire grin, as his physically-fit-for-a-fifty-seven-year-old body stood in front of me at the door. "Come on in."

He ushered me in and closed the door behind him. The door clicked shut, and I stood inside the dim room with my feet frozen in place just inside the entry, afraid of the situation. The alarm bells were ringing in my head. *You shouldn't be*

*in here with him alone. He shouldn't be in his boxers.* Shoulds
lead to shame.

I was mortified. Although I was almost nineteen, I was slow
to develop physically. I felt like a twelve-year-old virgin,
stuck in a twelve-year-old frame with no body fat and no
boobs, but the brain of an intuitive and wise old grandma.
(My mom's nickname for me as a little girl was "Granny
Stace.") I sensed something didn't feel right, and I wanted
to run out of there screaming.

Instead, I stuck to the plan that had taken me all day to
build up the courage to follow. "I want to be on the 4oo
medley relay." I paused, scared, but continued on. "I noticed
today in practice that Kristy was also doing relay starts. I'm
worried I'm not gonna be on it."

"Sweetheart," he used the term of endearment from his
Southern upbringing that made my nerves stand on end. It
felt patronizing, demeaning, and sexist. "You don't worry
about that. You just do what you need to do, and you *will* be
on that relay." He patted my shoulder and my skin crawled.

"Okay, thank you." I left the room as fast as he could say,
"Good night."

"Ugh! That was so creeeeeepy!" I shuddered the yuck off of
me when I returned to our room.

"What'd he say?" my roommate excitedly wondered.

"He said, 'Don't you worry about it.'" I laughingly imitated his voice, trying to make light of an inappropriate situation. "He said I'd be on the relay if *I did what I needed to do.*"

"Okay, so you're good."

"I guess." I laughed it off, but inside I was apprehensive and disgusted with myself, *and* him, for putting me in that situation in the first place.

Looking back, I wish my forty-year-old voice could have stood up for my nineteen-year-old self. I *wouldn't* have walked into his room. I would have asked him to put some pants on and talk to me in the hallway. My assertiveness developed from the experiences that shaped me to defend myself when needed. But I didn't know how to defend myself then. I held my breath often and didn't use my voice. I stayed silent and ran from uncomfortable situations.

How do we give others the confidence and space to use their voices when they know intuitively that something is wrong? Saying "no" and setting healthy boundaries is a skill that needs to be taught, modeled, and practiced. The most significant lesson you can learn is how to take your power back when someone of authority steals it from you. How do you heal when someone hurts you and not remain a victim?

# Dystopia

## September 15, 2000, Age 19

"Imagine there's no heaven...it's easy if you try." [22] The Olympic athletes sang along to the melodious sound of John Lennon's voice as it serenaded us. His message of a unified hope filled my heart with joy, as I grinned from ear to ear.

"Imagine all the people...living for today. Ah..."[23]

The scene was more than I could ever have imagined. The twinkling lights of 110,000 people holding candles surrounded us like fireflies in the dark night. I took in the opening ceremonies of the Sydney Olympics as I stood on the field next to famous tennis champions Venus and Serena Williams. My parents were somewhere in the crowd, experiencing this energetic shift in the world toward all that is good. Not only had all the athletes on the field worked to live the Olympic motto of *Citius, Altius, Fortius*—faster, higher, stronger—we were also a part of the same family now: Olympians.

Nearly four billion people from 220 countries were watching on television. I felt like I was at the center of the universe brightened with infinite stars...so small, yet so complete, unified as one in an overwhelming energy of love and light.

This was my absolute favorite memory of the games.

And then the fire water happened...

The Olympic flame, a forever fire that is never extinguished, was brought into the stadium by the traditional torch relay. To celebrate one hundred years of women's participation in the Olympics, famous Australian Olympic female champions passed the torch through the stadium. The final handoff was to Cathy Freeman, a two-time Australian Olympic sprinter who won a silver medal in the '96 games and would go on to win the 400-meter sprint as Olympic champion a few days later.

She was dressed in a shining white bodysuit, a turquoise water-like design from the gold medals at the games ran down the length of her side. She dramatically walked the orange flame burning bright up a long flight of stairs into a circular pool of deep blue water filled by the continuous illuminated staircase waterfall from above. She walked into the middle of the water, slowly lowered the flame to the surface, and ignited a circular cauldron of fire around her feet. The ring of fire that burned blue at the bottom to orange ombré at the dancing tips levitated up out of the water and above Cathy's head as it ascended the staircase waterfall. When it reached the pinnacle, it rested on a silver pedestal above the stadium. The sky immediately lit up with fireworks that boomed with each explosion of light. That was my cue to run.

I ran through the multitude of statuesque bodies staring frozen at the blazing sky. I vividly remember the long shadows cast by the still figures in awe of the spectacle—I felt like time had frozen them. I knew I had to reach the athlete transport area first, or I wouldn't get back to the Olympic Village for hours. I had to outrun 110,000 spectators, 12,687 performers, and athletes from 199 countries. In fact, only a handful of swimmers had decided to attend the opening ceremonies because our coaching staff had encouraged us to skip it so we wouldn't ruin our taper (a form of planned rest before performing that prepares muscles for ultimate exertion). *There's no fucking way I'd miss this!* I thought to myself as my strong, muscular legs carried me to the first bus in line. *That was so worth it!* I sat down on the front seat of the coach bus and giggled like I had just gotten away with something. I felt like the true champion of champions, having outwitted them all.

But truth is subjective.

The morning of the 100 breaststroke prelims, I felt off. I was so nervous. The routine I reflexively performed to put me in a meditative state and help my nerves at every championship meet wasn't working. I was aware of every little thing. Cognition took over my body, and I felt a premonition of doom I couldn't shake.

I was doing what Eric Wunderlich had warned me about. I was watching everyone else around me: The French swimmers who were smoking cigarettes under the bleachers of the warm-down pool. The South African coaches yelling at their swimmers to improve their starts. The synchronized swimmers walking around with gel in their hair and performance makeup caked onto their porcelain doll-like painted faces. It was surreal. And I felt disconnected from this world. It was nothing I had imagined.

To prepare for trials to make the Olympic team, I visualized my race with a stopwatch in my hand every night lying in bed for three years. I knew my stroke rate by heart, my number of strokes per lap. I could get within $1/10^{th}$ of a second from my goal every time: 1:06.10. That was the world record, and I wanted it. The human body doesn't know the difference between visualization and actual movement at the cellular level. The neurons are still firing when you think about movement. Dr. David Hamilton explains it this way:

[T]he fact that the brain processes imaginary as if it were real–that allows sports people to benefit from visualization practices. Several studies have shown that players can improve on their golf shots, tennis strokes, net shots in basketball, ice skating, football, or just about anything. Studies have shown people increasing their muscle strength by imagining themselves flexing muscles or lifting weights. In a study, for example, at the Lerner Research Institute in Cleveland, imagining flexing the little finger for 15 minutes daily for 3 months was shown to increase muscle strength by 35%...and the volunteers hadn't even lifted a finger.[24]

Owen Eastwood beautifully describes that "our ability to imagine is central to the human condition. When we vision, either seeing or imagining, and each time we consistently return to the vision, we are hardwiring neural pathways. Put another way, we are creating forward memories."[25] I visualized swimming at trials and making the team over and over and over again. It felt easy and natural because I had created such a strong forward memory to make the team. But my singular focus became a double-edged sword. It had the ability to help me and hurt me: I had focused all my energy to visualize making the team, but I never visualized swimming and winning at the Olympics. I hadn't been here before in person or in my mind. And I was fucked.

## September 17, 2000, Age 19

In prelims, I walked from the ready room to the blocks with the other seven swimmers, all total strangers, feeling uncertain and afraid. From behind my lane, I looked at the pool, and the end zoomed out away from me like a special effect in a movie. It looked one thousand meters long, unfamiliar and daunting. Unlike at trials, where I felt the presence of everyone supporting and surrounding me, here I felt isolated and far away from anyone or anything I knew.

Off the block, at the start, I watched the girl next to me dive in and gain a body length on me after the first pull down.

*How is she so far ahead?!* I thought as I tried to race her. But I was watching her race and not swimming mine. I ended up placing seventeenth, adding time from my trials time and not making it back to the semifinals that night.

Walking away from the pool and into the hall to grab my things, I placed my head in my towel and started to cry. My body shook with despair. My worst fear had come true. My opportunity to swim again was gone. There was no way the coaches would place me on the 400 medley relay now. Not after that performance. I had choked. Hard.

I couldn't talk about that race for ten years. I didn't want to watch it or think about it ever again. A decade later, my husband encouraged me to watch it with him. "I would love to see it. Don't you want to see it?" he pleaded.

I held in my hands the VHS tape that was given to each athlete by NBC. The broadcasting network owned the rights to the games, and nothing was digitized yet. The tape was the only proof of how much of a loser I felt like I was in that moment. But my husband was persuasive, and he had worn me down.

"Okay," I agreed.

As we watched the race, the picture cut to the underwater shot after the dive. I watched as the girl next to me took three short, quick dolphin kicks under the bubbles from the dive. In 2000, the rules for breaststroke did not allow any dolphin kicks off the start or turns.

"Did you see that!?" I asked my husband. "Rewind it! I have to see that again." And, sure enough, watching it more closely the second time, I saw what I couldn't believe. She had cheated. The officials had missed her surreptitious move.

"Are you kidding me!? She cheated! I can't believe it!" I exclaimed. And then the puzzle pieces came together. That is how she got so far ahead of me off the start. She qualified for sixteenth place that day and bumped me out of a second swim. I couldn't change the past, and at that point, it didn't matter to anyone else what had happened. But it mattered to me. I was grateful for the clarity. The darkness that surrounded that race lifted just a little.

That race, however, was only the beginning of the descent into the deep from my Olympic experience.

## September 22, 2000, Age 19

"That motherfucker!" My roommate threw one of her pillows across the room and fell into her bed, screaming into the mattress and punching the pillow that remained. In the three weeks that I had spent with her, I'd only seen her act with grace and composure. She was truly the most gorgeous-souled human. So this out-of-character response created a heightened sense of awareness and adrenaline in me.

In a team meeting minutes before we left for the 800 free relay Olympic finals night, the coaches announced the chosen participants for the relay. My roommate was rightfully upset because she wasn't on it, and no one had told her prior to the meeting. Richard had convinced her not to swim the 200 freestyle at Olympic Trials even though she was the fastest in the country in that event. The 200 individual medley (IM) was the same day as the 200 free. He had told her to focus on winning the 200 IM, and he promised her a spot on the 800 free relay at the Olympics.

She had rightfully earned her spot as the fastest swimmer in the country in the 200 free, but USA swimming doesn't choose swimmers for events based on who is fastest that season. The roster is chosen only from the finals swim at trials of that event. If she didn't swim the 200 free, it would allow for another girl to go for the relay and increase the roster. However, that sixth-place finisher could possibly not swim if another swimmer (who was the fastest, like my roommate) hadn't qualified at trials but was placed on the relay as promised. None of this was communicated to the athletes, which was problematic and created confusion and conflict.

I watched my roommate lose her shit, and my stomach dropped. This obviously was a moment of grief, and once trust is lost, it's almost impossible to get it back. I guessed I was next: False promises. No integrity. Loss. *What is happening?!* I wondered. I had to talk to Dave.

Dave was shocked when I told him what had happened. He had been exploring Darling Harbour in Sydney and had missed the discussion of who would be chosen for the relay. He was an assistant coach for the women's team and would have contributed a meaningful perspective to the discussion, had he been included.

"Dave," I said, "you *have* to talk to Richard. He promised me I'd be on that relay. There's no way he's going to put me on it if he did the same thing to my roommate! He *lied* to her, and I'm sure he *lied* to me. Also, Kristy did a time trial today in the 100 breaststroke in the warm-up pool. She wants that spot, and Kristy's coach and Richard are friends."

Dave threw his hands up in the air, to stop my rant and to comfort me. "Okay, I'll talk to him," he said. He didn't like conflict and avoided it if possible, but like a parent who cares for their child, he saw me hurting.

And he defended me.

"Richard, at this point, your integrity is in question," he said. "You promised Staciana she would be on that relay, so you need to put her on it. It's simple." Thank God Dave had my back. I wanted to redeem myself and get a second chance to swim faster. I wanted to contribute to the team in a positive way, and I wanted to win a gold medal.

After Richard's disingenuous actions were in question, he decided to put me on the morning relay for prelims. I swam faster than in my individual race, and my team qualified for finals. This gave the four other women who would swim it at night more rest to swim fresh. This was a common practice and allowed all eight of us to earn a gold medal from the games.

The night relay not only won—they broke the world record. I was fortunate to be deemed a part of the team and earn a medal. The most frequent question that you are asked when you return from the Olympics is "Did you get a gold medal?" And the sting if you don't come back with the greatest accomplishment in the world for your sport hurts every time. I could say, with a sense of relief and pride, "Yes, I did."

On the train later that week, some of our teammates were consoling Kristy.

"Is she okay?" I asked my teammate.

"No, she's upset because Richard promised her she would be on that relay."

"Are you kidding me?! He promised me too," I said. "What an asshole."

He had played us both. I couldn't believe it. We were pawns in his chess game. I should have used my voice and talked to Kristy about the situation before the relay. Our communication could have uncovered the manipulation. Positive communication can heal and prevent injury altogether. However, our silence allowed us to be manipulated and caused long-lasting, traumatic pain. Thankfully, Kristy and I didn't let this deception and manipulation ruin our friendship. We helped each other through conversations and shared experiences long after this difficult moment in our lives.

The coaches making the decisions had no idea the repercussions of their words and actions on us. Humans thrive in community and collaboration. But this situation was the opposite. The "win at all costs" mentality, which pitted us against each other in an archaic war game, negatively affected the athletes. The gold medals we won came at a price. An athlete's mental health and self-worth commonly correlate to their performance. If you take away the opportunity to perform, you take away that person's identity, and their self-worth plummets. Although I swam on the relay and earned a gold medal, my mental health was suffering. I had imagined the Olympics as a utopia, and the dystopian reality sent me into a deep, dark depression.

# POS Syndrome

## After the Games, 2000, Age 19

"You can dance, you can jive, having the time of your life. Ooh, see that girl, watch that scene, digging the dancing queen!"[26] We all sang along with hands in the air to the ABBA song and cheered on our teammate while she stood on the stage of the Home Bar and danced with her gold medal around her neck, arms spread out wide in a victory pose at the dance club in downtown Sydney. But like myself, the party for her was only on the outside. Our heavy souls were hurting. Our partying masked the pain.

Partying felt like something we had to do to rightfully finish out our Olympic experience. The swimming competition was the first two weeks of the games, so we had another week to celebrate before the closing ceremonies. And we partied.

Australia was the perfect place to party if you were a swimmer. The country loved swimming the way the U.S.

loves American football. It was the national pastime. A plethora of fifty-meter pools dotted the neighborhoods, similar to basketball courts or soccer fields in the U.S. It was incredible. As I watched Ian Thorpe's eight-foot face pass by me on the side of a bus, I thought, *I was born in the wrong country to be a swimmer.* The Australian swimmers were the national sports heroes, and I was reaping the rewards of our sport association. We all were.

When we returned home, the parties continued. Everyone wanted to celebrate with an Olympian—and there were many Cal student-athletes who had become Olympians that summer. When we returned to Berkeley, we partied like gods. The alcohol flowed freely, and deep bonds were made when the social walls disappeared during each drunk encounter. I cherished the camaraderie it created among us. But my body did not. Weeks of binge drinking caused me to gain weight and lose sleep, and it worsened my depression. I had stopped exercising for weeks and was feeling the withdrawal from all the feel-good neurotransmitters that consistent intense exercise creates in an athlete's body.

Also, the newfound fame made me question my relationships.

"Hey, that girl behind you..." I overheard two guys talking at a party one fall evening. They were drunk and obnoxious and had no clue how loudly they were talking over the music. "She's a gold medalist. I wanna fuck 'er."

"Fuck, yeah. Then you'll be part of the gold-medal club. It's like the mile-high club, but with Olympians."

*Ugh*, I thought. I was disgusted with them. Who could I trust now that I was famous for my accolades? Who liked me for *me*, and who was just drawn to me by the magnetism of the gold medal? My distrust in the goodness of humanity started at the games and was growing stronger with each superficial encounter.

To make matters worse, my body started to break down. I'd missed the proper buildup of conditioning the Cal swim team had participated in for the previous ten weeks while I was experiencing the Olympics, bingeing on free McDonald's three times a day in the Olympic village, and not training. Athletes spend years training for the Olympics, often only to mistakenly change all their habits as soon as the games are over. I tried to jump into hard winter training while I was out of shape and ended up bulging discs in my back from a cross-training ergometer practice. I had missed the lesson on proper technique, and my poor form caused an injury. My mind thought I could do anything, but my body said, "Fuck you!"

My injury and depression from lack of exercise and alcohol use led to more self-destructive behavior, and without guidance, I was lost. I grieved for the person I'd been before the games: innocent, hopeful, and naive. I grieved for the lost sense of self. If I remained injured and couldn't swim, who was I without swimming? And whom could I trust? I isolated myself more with each passing day, not attending class due to an Olympic waiver and struggling to attend practice with my injury. I felt alone.

This depression led me to research and publish my findings about Post-Olympic Stress (POS) Syndrome during my undergraduate studies at Cal. I decided to call these common problems POS Syndrome because I felt like a piece of shit. I knew I needed help.

After I returned home from the games, it took me two years to slowly swim up from the depths of the darkness. I had a fear of competing. How would I ever live up to the expectations of that accomplishment?

## Spring 2002, Age 20

"I'll tell you about Post-Olympic Stress Syndrome," my friend said, looking at me with his gorgeous, intense blue eyes and wide smile. "I got two DUIs, flipped a car, and got arrested before I realized I had a problem."

Two years after our Sydney experience together, we sat in the cafeteria of the U.S. Olympic Training Center in Colorado Springs during a national team camp. I was writing my undergraduate thesis on POS Syndrome, a term I had created based on my research synthesizing PTSD and Maslach's burnout theory. Dr. Christina Maslach was my thesis mentor at UC Berkeley, and I was correlating her longitudinal quantitative study with my qualitative research documenting athletes' anecdotal accounts of injury and depression after the Olympics. POS Syndrome wasn't talked about, and there was no support—yet everyone I talked to in my circle of Olympians had experienced some form of it.

I wanted to understand the phenomenon, and I wanted to help myself and others. The commonalities among us were too similar to ignore. The outpouring of stories I collected revealed a systemic problem. There was an inherent structure of support from National Governing Bodies (NGBs) to ensure athletes could achieve greatness and make the Olympic Games. Unfortunately, at the time, there was no protocol or standard operating procedure to support the Olympians after they finished competing.

In the early 2000s, mental health was still a topic people didn't generally discuss, and it's common not to recognize you're depressed when you're struggling. It took someone else from the outside looking in to shed light on the darkness within me. I didn't know how to ask for help. I felt alone. But I wasn't alone. The more I researched and connected with others struggling, the more I accepted the normalcy of the syndrome.

Through communication and collaboration with a good friend, Adam Lee, I expanded my perspective on the issue. Adam competed internationally in water polo and had years of experience coaching the sport at the club and junior college levels. He had compiled his own qualitative research, interviewing 125 athletes at all levels who struggled with the same issues of POS Syndrome: depression, injury, substance use and abuse, isolation, and loss of community and sense of self. Based on his findings, he asked me to consider broadening the scope of concern to include *all* athletes and their struggles to transition out of competing, a subject that needs further qualitative and quantitative research to acknowledge and support them.

The level at which they practiced or competed didn't matter. What mattered was they felt like pieces of shit when they took a break or retired from competition. They made choices that took them down a rabbit hole of self-destructive behavior, which reinforced their self-deprecating thoughts.

For athletes transitioning away from sport, there are few resources or practices to educate and support them. My wish is to encourage and continue further research, in addition to cultivating a network of people who are interested in advancing this field of study to create a program for the population of former athletes who need to thrive in life, both during and after their athletic careers.

Like grief, people must normalize the feelings associated with the letdown of athletic pursuit when they stop training and competing. As Eastwood explains, when discussing the Proteas team he worked with,

> The Proteas' inability to sustain excellence makes sense from a hormonal point of view. Our dopamine system is anticipatory. We receive bursts in the pursuit of a goal rather than on attainment of it. These bursts increase when the outcome is uncertain as opposed to guaranteed. This explains why we can feel so flat immediately after a major event or performance.[27]

Education, awareness, and collective support will help prepare athletes to ride the waves of fame, identity crisis, disillusionment, and grief layered within the athletic experience and life after competitive sport. The exercises and practices that I explain in Part Five, later in this book, are a great starting point for athletes and anyone else struggling with grief and trauma. These activities are based on the findings of positive psychology and my own experience. More resources can also be found at the back of this book.

Another fascinating area of study is being conducted by Erin Cafaro, who is a clinical psychology doctoral student at the Wright Institute at UC Berkeley as well as a two-time Olympic gold medalist for USA rowing in the 2008 and

2012 Olympics. She is conducting a quantitative research study about athletes' lives during and after athletics and the factors that play a part in their athletic success and mental health outcomes when transitioning away from athletics. Her clinical psychology studies have focused on chronic pain, neuropsychology, and cognitive rehabilitation. She continues to consult and learn from various performance communities, including athletes, military personnel, first responders, and business professionals. She talks about the importance of protective factors that help prevent mental health struggles, including but not limited to a supportive network of medical professionals and resources, therapy-based practices, and medication when needed to help with the transition away from sport—not only for career success but also for the ability to thrive in the next adventures of life.

Along with the practices stated above, mentorship from those with similar firsthand experiences is vital to supporting athletes and people in grief. You don't know what you don't know. Shared wisdom from experience (like this book!) brings comfort to first-timers dealing with any challenging situation. The support network may not prevent the fall completely, but it will cushion the landing and help you bounce back, strengthening your resilience through understanding and grace.

# Trials 2.0

*"Our greatest glory is not in never falling, but in rising every time we fall."*

—Oliver Goldsmith[28]

## July 2004, Age 22

"One-oh-seven-one-zero. One-oh-seven-one-zero." I read the time off the scoreboard twice, 1:07.10, as I stared in awe at the outcome of peak physical training and mental preparation. I felt so much joy. I had not swum a best time since the Olympic Trials four years earlier. Now, in the prelims of trials in 2004 in Long Beach, California, I was the fastest in the country.

My time was half a second off the world record, 1/10th of a second off the American record, and the fastest time of the morning by a full second, which is an eternity in the sprint event. It gave me the confidence going into finals to make my second Olympic team the following night.

But as I had learned in the past, words are impactful, and my coach's choice of words this time around changed the course of my future.

## Twelve Months Earlier: July 2003, Age 21

After I graduated from Cal in 2003, I went back to train with Dave again at Irvine NOVAS. He had a group of twenty-five postgrads who were all pushing the limits of training protocols. Dave decided to offer a training regimen on a four-day cycle: three days of work (double practice, single practice, double practice) followed by one day of rest. Our job was to train, and it didn't matter what day of the week it fell on. This unprecedented training cycle increased the amount of rest every twenty-eight days.

In one month, we got seven days of rest versus four. Because of this intentional increase in rest, I worked hard, recovered faster, and grew stronger mentally and physically. I trained six hours on double days and two hours on single days, stuck to a firm nutrition plan, and soaked up the sun. The seven-day work cycle would fatigue me to the point of counterproductivity, because all I knew how to do at practice was grind. The four-day work cycle was perfect for someone who didn't know how to rest. I worked until I felt complete muscle failure every day. This increase in forced rest allowed for more work. I was a professional swimmer (being paid in pennies) and living out my dreams. I was one fast, sexy, tan, rested motherfucker.

"I want to break the world record in the 100 breaststroke," I joyfully told Jessica Hardy. She and I stood face to face at practice during a goal-setting activity that Dave had asked us to participate in. We had to look a partner in the eye and verbalize our goals for the season. Having an accountability partner would increase our chances of success. Jes repeated my goal back to me: "I want to break the world record in the 100 breaststroke." I smiled, and she smiled back. Same goal, same event, very different places in our swimming careers—this was going to be fun.

I loved racing in practice. I almost always raced the guys, because they were more often willing to race. Dave Denniston and I gave each other shit every day in practice to make each other better. I teased him about his weak-ass kick, and he teased me about my lack of upper body strength. We pushed each other. We fed off each other's competitiveness. And we dragged Jes along with us.

She was sixteen, and I was twenty-one. She was in high school, and I had graduated from college. She saw me as a mentor, and I treated her with love and encouragement every day in practice. So having the same goal wasn't problematic. We would make each other better with the constant competition.

Our coach, Dave Salo, knew Jes had potential to achieve greatness. He wanted to encourage her progress with small victories to increase her self-confidence.

Reflecting back on the pre-swim speech before the 100 breaststroke final at trials, I knew intuitively this is why he said what he said. He brought us together after our warm-up, and we stood in a close circle of trust. The wrinkles at the corners of his eyes, from years of sunshine and joy, smiled at us as he shared the plan, looking at us both with resolution on his face: "I want Jes to touch first at the 50, and I want Staciana to touch first at the 100."

And I complied. I was loyal. I trusted him. And we were a team: we would do it together. Nothing could stop us.

Except, I was never a "back-halfer." I always took it out as fast as I could. I held the American Record in the 50 breast at one point in my career from a 50-split while swimming the 100 breast.

You learn more from your failures than you do from your successes. You can glean success from failure if you learn something from it each time. It's when you stop growing, reflecting, and adapting that you truly fail.

In our culture, it is easy to feel like a failure if you don't win. In 2004 at trials, I didn't swim my own race in the 100 breaststroke. Jes went out faster than me at the 50, as Dave had suggested, and I couldn't come back with enough speed to place first or second. Five girls went into the wall at the same time. I finished fourth, and Jes finished fifth. I didn't swim to my own strengths; she did. Neither of us were going. I felt like a failure.

In 2000, Dave had asked me to close my eyes at the end of my race and ask myself if I had done everything I could. In 2000, the answer was yes, and I had made the team. I reiterated this same question in my head when I touched the wall in 2004, knowing the question was important for my own peace, no matter the outcome. A small but firm voice quietly answered back, *No*.

Seeing a "4" by my name on the scoreboard when I turned around in 2004 enraged me. I was so angry for letting someone else influence my race strategy. But I couldn't blame Dave. My anger was directed within. I had not swum to my own selfish competitive potential. I had put Jes's perceived needs before my own, and I had sacrificed an opportunity to shine on the Olympic stage. No one had beaten my time from prelims. I knew I was the fastest in the country, but I still felt like a loser. I wasn't going to Athens.

I wanted to throw my goggles and storm off the deck with my head down, feeling ashamed. However, that quiet but firm voice inside said to me, *Don't you dare*. I thought of all the people in the stands supporting me who sacrificed so much to help me get to this moment. I would honor them by holding my head high, smiling and acknowledging them

with a wave. *Don't tarnish their sacrifices with selfish feelings.*
The internal voice spoke to me with deep clarity.

When I looked up to wave along the fifty-meter walk of
shame from the starting end to the warm-down pool, I was
shocked. All of the littles in the front row were cheering and
waving papers for an autograph. Smiling through gritted
teeth, I thought, *Can they not see the scoreboard? I didn't
make it. What a fuckin' LOSER!* My internal dialogue was
nasty. But the littles didn't feel that way. They just wanted
to connect with me, no matter what. I realized I was already
shining on their stage.

For the four years prior, whenever someone asked for an
autograph or recognized me as an Olympian, I'd stop and
take the time to connect. How I acted as a person, valuing
connection, defined me more than the medal around my
neck. And this moment solidified this lesson. I had lost my
opportunity to get another Olympic medal, but I had gained
insight about what it means to succeed.

# PART 3: EARTH

*"Grief and unexpected joy live in a doorway where there is no time or distance."*

—Rumi[29]

# Closer

## Summer 2002, Age 20

The beat of the song pounded in my chest. We danced in an animalistic ritual, driven by alcohol and testosterone. Candlelight flickered to the rhythm in the dark room, illuminating the small group of friends who surrounded us. We had started an impromptu dance party in his bedroom, which looked like an orgy. Except, everyone was clothed. I leaned against him, my ass in his crotch, my head against his chest. His six-foot-five frame and long arms wrapped around me, making me feel small and feminine. I pulled up my thin black tank top halfway and tucked it into my bra, to let the heat escape from deep within my body. I felt a flame ignite anytime we were close to each other. His fingers traced the sweat that slowly dripped down my abs, until he reached the hem of my low-cut jeans. He teased me, lightly moving his fingertips back and forth just inside my waistline. Grinding to the music, he leaned in closer, whispering the words of the Nine Inch Nails song "Closer" in my ear: "I wanna fuck you like an animal..." I could feel his warm breath on my neck. "...I wanna feel you from the inside."[30]

"Yes," I thought in my drunken haze.

Sensing my willingness, he pushed me face down, bent over the bed, and leaned over against me. He grabbed my stomach and rubbed it from bra line to panty line in one strong smooth movement. He pulled me into him while his body moved rhythmically over mine, thrusting into me with each bass drumbeat. I moaned, coming in my jeans, then sank into the bed.

*Holy shit!* I thought, silent and awestruck at the power of his touch. An explosion of sexual energy released, making me feel things I had never felt before. *Who comes fully dressed? What the fuck?*

And I knew I wanted him. All of him. He knew it too. You couldn't deny the chemistry between us.

He whispered in my ear, "That's all you get," and sauntered out of the room with an impish grin.

"Ugh...you asshole," I whispered into the duvet cover, frustrated, but internally smiling at the game he was playing. He left me wanting more. His name was Brett Winfield.

What does it mean to be loved by somebody? Is it a feeling? Is it an act?

The definition of love has evolved many times over in my life. As a little girl, love was expected: the unconditional love from my parents, the protective love from my older sister, the sisterly love for my younger brothers, and the love from and for God. My parents exemplified their faith through prayer. We would chant together, "God, please protect our family. Keep us well and happy. Give us the strength, the courage, and the love to do the right thing. Amen." This nightly prayer embedded in my brain the belief that God loves and protects us, giving us the strength and courage to do hard things.

There is a rite of passage that everyone must go through to understand *chosen* love. To be loved by someone who isn't your family is a paradigm shift. I was intoxicated the first time I felt this love. My first boyfriend taught me what it felt like to be loved. We were compatible in many ways—both insanely driven to become the best athletes in the world, balancing rigorous training with challenging academic pursuits. We found a rhythm and balance to our dreams and desires quickly. We dated for a year, and he gave me so much confidence in myself as someone who *could* be loved.

Unfortunately, our love didn't last. I didn't love him the way he loved me. I loved the idea of being in love, but I couldn't be my true self with him. I was ready to leave the cocoon and become a social butterfly, gaining confidence in my ability to interact with others. Most swimmers lack these social skills from too many hours staring at the bottom of a pool. My boyfriend wanted to hang out with just me. I wanted to hang out with everyone else. He wanted to get married, and I wanted to dance at the bar with my girlfriends. He told me I was perfect. I knew I wasn't. I wanted someone to love me for all my imperfections. We broke up, and I regret hurting him. But my fear of losing this chosen love was overcome by the light of intuition. His love helped me believe in the possibility of being loved by someone other than my family—I just didn't want that love to be from him.

And the quiet voice inside whispered, *But, maybe from Brett...*

Brett surreptitiously groped me the first time our paths crossed my sophomore year of college when I returned home from the Olympics. I had meticulously selected an outfit to show off my body at a college athlete party: a backless cheetah-print crop top and low-waisted tight black pants that hugged every inch of my lower half. I wanted to be spotted. I was growing into my sexuality, yet struggling with my own mental demons and self-worth. I found a release in dressing provocatively and partying.

Brett was on a recruiting trip to Cal and stood against a wall at the party, next to his friend. Brett's hand was magnetized to my breaststroke booty, and he smacked it as I walked past him onto the dance floor. When I turned around, not knowing who it was, Brett's friend caught my eye: a beautiful specimen, brown curly hair, dark sinister eyes, and broad shoulders. I knew I wanted to dance with him. I grabbed his hand and pulled him into the crowd of people, bumping and gyrating to '90s hip-hop. We danced as Brett watched. He stood against the wall, wearing a cowboy hat low across his forehead. I never saw his face and had no idea he was the one who groped me. (In Brett's true style, he didn't reveal this fun fact until we were already much in love and married five years later.)

My second encounter with Brett was more memorable. He sat next to me in a sports sociology lecture our junior year and started doodling yellowfin tuna and smiley faces on my notebook. I thought, *Who is this guy?* He was tall, with veiny forearms, strong muscular legs, and gorgeous, vibrant turquoise eyes. He wore his hat backward, which made me look twice every time. One day in class, he asked if we could study together. With some hesitation, I agreed. I was often annoyed with him, thinking he was just using me to do the reading and tell him the answers, which was partially true. Other useless crushes had used me for similar things in the past, and I wasn't falling for his ulterior motives disguised as charm.

One warm spring night at another party, Brett pissed me off enough that I told him how I felt. Earlier in the night, in the privacy of my own bedroom, I had done what any flat-chested girl who wants to feel provocative does. First, I stuck "chicken cutlets" (the fake stick-on boobs models use in photo shoots) onto the bottom of my breasts. Next, I duct-taped them together. Then, I added a push-up bra over the top. Finally, I threw on a low, tight-fitting royal blue corset top, so my boobs were kissing my chin. This ridiculous process created the illusion of cleavage, which I thought would make me feel more confident and attractive.

Standing back to back, Brett and I were talking to a tight crowd of friends, and he kept bumping into me. I was annoyed as always with his oversize personality and confidence, so I turned around and gave him a nasty look. I was clearly growing into my sexuality and testing boundaries with clothing. Brett looked at me, then looked down at my chest and said, "Put those things away!" with a shit-eating grin on his face. I was mortified! *How dare he speak to me like that!* His charming smile and harsh words powered by truth rocked me to my core. He was calling my shit out! No sugar-coating. It made me hate him even more. Of course, I wanted the attention, but I hated his boldness in saying it so blatantly.

The next day in lecture, I let him have it. For the first time, I used my voice to defend myself. And it turned him on.

"I hope you were drunk on Saturday night," I started, "because you were a total asshole! I can't believe the things you said."

He gazed at me with a look of confusion, empathy, and attraction. Truly dumbfounded, he replied, "What? What did I say? I don't remember."

"You said, 'Put those things away!'" I mimicked his rude tone and gestures, throwing my hands toward his chest.

He grinned and chortled, "I remember that! I wasn't being rude; I was being honest."

"Ugh! You are such an asshole." His honesty helped me share my authentic and raw feelings. I wasn't holding anything back. I couldn't believe him. He really had some nerve.

He looked at my eyes filled with pain and backed down. "I didn't mean to hurt your feelings."

"Maybe not, but you did!"

"Well, I'm sorry," he said.

The rest of the spring and all summer, we hung out often. He called me to study, barbeque, and surf. We became best friends, and my love for Brett grew stronger the more we shared food, words, and time. Brett and I both grew up in the ocean of Southern California. Every summer was spent at the beach playing in the waves. Brett had worked on the fishing boats since he was twelve, as a pinhead, deckhand, first mate, and, by age eighteen, finally captain, to save money for college. But in the summer of 2002, we both independently and serendipitously decided to stay in the Bay Area for different reasons.

However, we both missed the beach terribly. His blue Ford Explorer often packed in a crew of swimmers and rowers to speed down the 101 to Pacifica, a forty-five-minute drive from Berkeley. We would surf and play in the ocean whenever we had the chance. He and his four rowing roommates would host barbecues after the beach, and we would all hang out together. He was so cute that I couldn't help but look at him often.

Dr. Beth-Sarah Wright describes the etymology of the word "respect" when she asks us to look at the dignity of every human being. When broken down into its parts, "spect" (look) and "re" (again), the word means "to look again." She explains that we see something different when we pause and take another look. We might see something we value.[31] The more I watched Brett, the more I grew to love his heart and respect him for his generosity with his time and his resources. He wanted to make people laugh, cook great food for them, and spend time together.

That first summer, he and I were at the beach in Pacifica, digging in the sand and playing like kids. He began to mold the sand into the shape of a boat. I watched as he carefully took his time to perfect the sides of the vessel with his rough rowing hands. He had shared details of his life: his love for the ocean, fishing adventures, running the boat as a captain in Newport. As he sculpted, he described the boat that funded his college tuition. It was called the *Amigo*. I couldn't help but think, as he formed it with love in front of me, *How appropriate*. I loved him as a friend...and maybe more.

As the song goes, "I wanna fuck you like an animal..."[32]

Alcohol makes my lips move. Thanks to my dad's genes, I get diarrhea of the mouth and kissy face the minute alcohol hits the blood-brain barrier.

Brett and his roommates learned this about me quickly that summer and jumped in like a band of big brothers. They insisted I stay overnight alone in their empty teammate's bed to protect me from myself. They also wanted to protect my boyfriend, who rowed on the same team but was gone for the summer, so I wouldn't cheat on him. They were true gentlemen who knew the pain of infidelity. Brett and I had many sleepovers that summer, staying up talking until all hours of the night, but never crossing the line physically. Brett was a man of honor. One night he confessed, "My last girlfriend cheated on me, and I would never do that to my teammate." I listened, agreed, and fell in love with him even more.

A premonition hit me like a lightning bolt at the end of the summer and scared the shit out of me. I saw us: me and Brett, clear as day, at the beach, running around playing with our two dogs. *What am I doing?!* I wondered. *I have a boyfriend. How can I be feeling so much love for this man? He's an asshole. We aren't even together. WE HAVEN'T EVEN KISSED!*

So, I did what any twenty-year-old girl would do in this situation: I ghosted him for a week. I avoided him at all costs, not wanting to confront the fact that I had feelings for him. I stopped answering his phone calls. I decided the best thing to do was to let the friendship go. Thankfully, Brett wouldn't. He kept calling, kept texting, and persisted until I gave in. "Fine, I'll meet you for coffee," I conceded.

We met at Caffè Strada, a beautiful coffee shop in Berkeley. When you walk into the cafe, you are surrounded by old Victorian white walls contrasted by the golden oak floor that glows from the morning light. You immediately feel a contact high from the espresso in the air. On the patio, the sunlight scatters through the green leaves that rustle in the breeze onto the people and students below. I felt smarter through osmosis, just sitting there absorbing the buzz of intellectual conversations happening all around me.

Brett was enticing that day. His backward sky-blue hat matched his gorgeous crystal-blue eyes. He sat down across from me and asked directly, "So what's up? Why have you been avoiding me?"

"Well..." I began.

He listened to me talk with intensity, leaning into every word with his thumb under his chin and index finger on his nose, framing a confident grin. I confessed my feelings for him. I admitted I liked him. I admitted I felt like I was cheating on my boyfriend. I admitted I had seen our lives together in the future with two dogs on the beach, which freaked me out.

Brett was a master chess player. He could see multiple steps ahead in any situation and knew the outcome of each choice. He was careful and calculated that day. I had no idea at the time, because I was never five steps ahead. I usually was in the present moment. He saw more, and he knew he would lose me if he admitted he liked me too. So instead, he laughed it off, saying, "You're crazy. We're just friends. Nothing more. I don't have feelings for you like that. I just wanna hang out. You're freaking out over nothing."

My ego was destroyed. I felt like a fool. But I was also relieved. I didn't have to lose my best friend.

Love is an act and a feeling. As humans, we choose to love. He and I chose to love each other. That reciprocated choice led to an honest friendship full of teasing, laughter, drive, passion, love, and pain.

# Death Dream

## Summer 2002, Age 20

The summer of 2002 was a season of shared secrets. The intentional walls that we built around us to hide imperfections during courtship didn't exist between Brett and me when we fell in love. We *weren't* dating. We weren't interested in each other—until we were. Shared secrets connected us. Sharing truths and vulnerabilities formed bonds stronger than we realized.

One summer evening, we lay in his bed, talking into the late hours of the night by moonlight. As my eyes started to close, he slid off the end of the bed and walked to his closet.

"You can't sleep in that," he said, referring to my going-out clothes. "I mean...*I* usually sleep naked." He shrugged his shoulders and threw up his hands. "But I'll keep my boardshorts on just in case you get any ideas," he teased as he threw me one of his perfectly folded T-shirts and removed his own from his chiseled torso. We were justifying the intimacy of words with physical barriers. I should have recognized the clear signs that we liked each other.

When he returned to bed, he placed a giant king-size pillow between us lengthwise.

"What are you doing?" I asked.

"This will keep *you* from touching me."

"Oh, okay, like I need that," I sneered in a silly voice.

"You know you do. You can't resist me."

"Bullshit! If *you* need 'Fort Knox' to keep your hands off *me*, go ahead. But I have no problem lying here and keeping my hands to myself."

I walked to his closet, stripped off my clothes behind the door, and slipped on his oversized T-shirt, giggling inside.

We lay there, on either side of Fort Knox, listening to Mazzy Star. His dark bedroom glowed from the magic of the moonlight illuminating the stained-glass window of the old Victorian house in the Northside neighborhood of Berkeley.

"I have to tell you something." His eyes grew dark and his voice serious, a strong contradiction to his usual jovial nature.

"Sure." I sat quietly, knowing silence was the best way to help someone reveal deep, vulnerable thoughts.

"I've never told anyone..."

I nodded, still listening.

"I had a dream when I was little that I would die at thirty-five."

I laughed out loud. "Ha! Well, the way you drive, I'm not surprised." I had experienced his reckless driving firsthand. He often would bump Ludacris and sing, "MOVE, BITCH, GET OUT DA WAY! GET OUT DA WAY, BITCH, GET OUT DA WAY!"[33] while swerving violently around cars for fun. I had also heard many stories of his friends and teammates making stupid decisions that should have landed them in jail or dead.

But the dream of his youth wasn't a joke for him. It was real and vivid and explicit. He refused to share the details of how he died in his dream, that night or any time after. He kept things close to his heart that he knew would hurt me. But he shared that he was living his life hard and fast, and not wasting a minute of it. He believed the dream.

As time passed, the death dream became a running joke in our relationship. We made decisions based on the idea that he was going to be dead before his thirty-sixth birthday. I'm sure there were times he regretted sharing this dream with me. I always tried to lighten up the dreaded premonition with humor. He would smile and laugh along on the inside.

Talk of the dream resurfaced five years into our marriage when we were debating having children. I'd always wanted three, while he wanted none. We sat on Marine Avenue of Balboa Island, sipping our ritual Starbucks, atop bubblegum-pink wrought-iron chairs in front of a beachy clothing boutique. I persuaded him with a cheeky smile, "What am I gonna do when you're dead at thirty-five? I'll need someone to remind me of you, so I'm not alone."

He returned the smile with a raised eyebrow. "You never knew me as a child. You have no idea what you're getting into."

"True, but I know you now. We would make some cute babies." I nodded, encouraging him.

"Well, that's true."

"Although..." I paused, reconsidering, "with your good looks and my sex drive, we might be in trouble if we have a girl."

"No shit."

# Mr. Midnight

## July 2009, Age 27

"Okay, so I have good news and bad news. Which do you want first?" Brett and I sat in the swanky Wellness Center at a private concierge's doctor's office who was in the business of medicine and making money. Dressed in a sharp black business suit, white collared shirt unbuttoned to her cleavage, and black stiletto heels, the doctor's tan skin and long, blonde hair confidently screamed, "I'm a badass and I know it!"

She was a fully licensed medical doctor who could run any test you wanted. She was renowned for her more natural approach to medicine and connections to unorthodox European laboratories for health and wellness research and testing capabilities. She offered everything from vitamin-C IV drips to a privately manufactured supplement store, as well as cosmetic procedures and more—everything to serve the high-paying clientele of South Orange County who wanted to stay healthy and look youthful at any age. And she didn't accept insurance. We were referred to her by a good friend who valued her untraditional opinion.

"Let's start with the bad news," Brett joked.

"Well, it seems from your blood work that you may have testicular cancer."

"Huh. What's the good news?"

"If you don't have testicular cancer, you might be pregnant," she remarked flippantly, knowing we were trying. Considering the limitations of the male species to procreate, the pregnancy would have been a miraculous achievement. "You have prolactin in your blood. This hormone is released so pregnant women can lactate. Obviously, you're not pregnant. The only other consideration is that you may have a brain tumor on your pituitary gland that is causing hormonal shifts in your body. How's your sex life?"

"Good," he said too quickly. "We are trying to get pregnant, so it's happening regularly."

"Yes, I understand you're having sex, but do you feel like you want to?"

"I mean...I guess?" Brett's voice raised with a guilty inflection as he looked at me like a little boy caught with his hand in the cookie jar.

"I only ask because your testosterone level's almost zero. I'm surprised that you're able to get an erection." She pulled no punches.

"Well, Mr. Midnight," he said, referring to his penis's nickname, "seems to be fine." He grinned, trying to make light of a shitty situation.

"I'd like you to have an MRI to give us more information. Best-case scenario, it's a brain tumor. Those are usually benign and can be fixed more easily than testicular cancer."

"Well, if it's between losing part of my brain or losing a ball or two, I guess I choose brain. There wasn't much there to start with." He was self-deprecatingly funny as always.

In 2008, our youth and drive helped push the limits of time and energy to sustain an expensive life in Southern California. We were both chasing our dreams of success in our fields of work and charging hard together. I was an assistant coach at the University of Southern California for the men's and women's swim teams. I loved coaching. It was a blast to guide and challenge the young swimmers. But the endless cycle of recruiting to replace the athlete turnover demolished a work-life balance. I decided to leave and teach at a private school in Los Angeles. They wanted me to coach their swim team and teach P.E. I wanted to start a family. The doors were wide open for a change, and I gratefully stepped through.

Brett was working for A.P. Møller – Mærsk, the global shipping company, out of the Long Beach port. We were in our late twenties, working fourteen- to sixteen-hour days, six, sometimes seven, days a week. The stress and long hours didn't help our sex life. He worked nights and weekends, so we only saw each other for small windows of time. After a year of negative pregnancy tests, we knew we needed medical advice. But the results were unexpected.

An MRI confirmed he had a microadenoma in his brain that had shifted the stalk of his pituitary gland. The natural hormonal signals were not reaching the end of the stalk to tell the male body *not* to release prolactin, which destroyed his sex drive.

He was referred to an incredible UCLA neurosurgeon who reassured us he would remove the tumor safely. "I have done it over one thousand times with a high success rate," he said. "I'll go through your nasal cavity, cut a segment out of your skull to reach the pituitary tumor, remove the tumor, and replace the bone that has been removed, cauterizing it back into place. There's minimal risk of brain damage, but you should be aware that brain surgery always involves some risk. Brett may come out losing function to walk, talk, etc. if anything happens unexpectedly." That was some serious shit to consider. We apprehensively scheduled the surgery.

During the same period of time, our desire to enter the overpriced housing market in Southern California created a manic search for a dream home. The great financial crisis of 2008 had devastated the global economy, and buying a house became a bit more complicated. Our over-asking-price offer on a short sale condo in Dana Point was risky because we would be upside down financially if we committed to it. They accepted our offer at the same time Brett's tumor was discovered.

The brain tumor not only shifted his pituitary stalk, but also our paradigm. "Fuck it!" we said.

We backed out of the offer on the condo, took our $10,000 savings for a down payment, and went on the best vacation of our lives to the Virgin Islands. We flew there right before his scheduled surgery and enthusiastically said, "Yes!" to every adventure, no matter the cost. The free rum shots that welcomed us when we deboarded the plane foreshadowed our week. We drank a fuck-ton of rum, sailed on the open ocean on the *Serendipity*, swam from black tip reef sharks, followed the biggest sea bass underwater for miles, partied with the locals, and dreamed of no responsibilities. We both implicitly knew that if he died during surgery, at least we had one last great adventure together.

I had learned early on in our relationship that Brett hated hospitals. Our first year of marriage, he worked three jobs, including running fishing charters for a six-pack out of Newport. On a shark-fishing charter, a thick-gauged hook mistakenly flew through the air and got stuck in the palm of his hand. Far out to sea, he ordered his deckhand to saw the hook in two while he applied pressure to it to keep it in place. They needed to remove it so they could keep fishing. To sterilize the wound, he placed his bleeding hand in a bucket of bleach, compartmentalizing the searing pain. When he returned home, he proudly showed me the pieces of the hook and his hand, saying, "You wouldn't believe what happened today."

The red streak running up the vein near the injury site made me nervous. I insisted he go to the hospital to get a tetanus shot. He refused.

A few days later, after many persuasive attempts and stubborn refusals, I called his grandma. You didn't mess with Granny. She had outlived two husbands, still walked eighteen holes of golf at age ninety-two, called the seventy-five-year-old hunchbacked women at her nursing home the "old ladies," and could put anyone, especially Brett, in his place. She made him go to the hospital with one phone call. As we sat in the hospital room, he fidgeted uncomfortably.

"What's your problem?!" I finally asked him.

He hesitated. "I hate needles," he solemnly admitted.

"Are you kidding me?!" I was shocked. "You can get a hook sawed off your hand and put your gaping wound in a bucket of bleach, but you're afraid of a needle?! How's that possible? Suck it up, buttercup!" I said, repeating back to him what he often said to me if I was struggling–it was firm, take-no-prisoners encouragement.

But his fear of hospitals was warranted when he had his brain surgery. When Brett came out of anesthesia, he wasn't able to speak.

"Brett, love, can you hear me? Squeeze my hand if you can hear me," I said.

He squeezed my hand and started to make moaning sounds. His words seemed mumbled, like he was unable to move his tongue properly.

The anticipatory fear inside me transformed to reality. *Does he have brain damage?* I wondered. *Did something unexpected happen?*

A minute passed as my fear took over and I wondered if I was going to have to take care of a vegetable.

But then, he slowly opened his eyes as a grin grew across his face. His gaze met mine, and he said, "I'm fine, stop worrying."

"You ASSHOLE!" I laughed, relieved, and slapped him on the shoulder.

"Ouch. Be careful, I'm fragile."

"Yeah, right."

During his recovery the first night, the nurses fucked up royally during shift change. He had a drain in his spine to reduce the cerebral spinal fluid (CSF) that was building up around his brain from the surgery. They neglected to check the drain after opening it and accidentally drained off too much CSF while I was in the shower.

"Babe, something's wrong," he complained as I walked out of the single stall bathroom. "I hear this bubbling noise inside my head, and it's pounding. It hurts so bad." I hurried out to the nurses' station and assertively asked for the charge nurse.

"Something's wrong with my husband. I think he needs help," I explained. She followed me back to the dark room and found the error. But the damage had been done.

It was touch and go all night, and I wondered if he was going to die. He had become unbearably light- and noise-sensitive. His moans throughout the night were real this time. The constant beeping and interruptions to check on him made it impossible for him to rest. Thankfully, slowly, his body began to recover, and after three days with no sleep, he asked to be discharged early. I didn't fight him. I knew he was miserable, and the body needs rest to recover. The nurses said it was okay to be discharged, as long as I was with him as his caretaker. I would have to monitor his fevers to make sure they didn't go above a certain temperature, in addition to helping him regain his ability to walk. I could call the emergency hospital line anytime to get advice or help. My family helped me cover our apartment windows in black trash bags to deal with his light sensitivity to keep him comfortable. I was terrified. I wasn't a nurse. *How am I supposed to keep him alive?* I wondered.

After seventy-two hours at home, and more than twenty phone calls to the emergency hospital line due to his recurring high fevers and vomiting, he started to improve, and I began to relax. Our short walks outside to help him regain his strength grew longer with each passing day. We laughed at his helplessness. The strongest man I knew needed me. And I was so happy to do it—scared shitless, but happy. He was alive. He was recovering. And he was still the most caring, loving asshole I knew.

The surgeon had advised us before surgery, "Once you recover, you will be chasing her around the bedroom like a thirteen-year-old boy. You will have a constant hard-on for a week or two. The uptake in testosterone does wonders for a man's sex drive. But it's important you refrain from having sex for four to six weeks. You need time to let your skull heal." Brett was a fast runner, and I wanted to be caught. Mr. Midnight was awake and ready to play. We lasted three weeks.

We were pregnant a month later.

# Stop Sign

## January 2015, Age 33

"I wanna go hike the Pulai waterfall this weekend together as a family. It's supposed to be beautiful," I commanded with a tinge of resentment, like a "threenager" asserting authority.

In the sixteen months that we had lived in Johor Bahru, Brett, Kyla, and I had traveled as often as we could outside of Malaysia. But we hadn't explored much of the wild jungle of our local city, and I was craving a free family adventure.

"Sure," Brett agreed, knowing I was on the verge of losing it.

We packed up Kyla's jogging stroller, which had seen thousands of miles of road in all different parts of the world. Her existence pushed us to keep going. We wanted to show her the amazing world we lived in. We refused to be the couple who had a baby and stayed home for convenience. She loved the stroller, a vehicle of adventure. It had gotten stuck deboarding a speed train in Amsterdam, wobbled on the 400 A.D. old-as-fuck cobblestone streets of Bruges, and avoided the donkeys and sheep on the sidewalks of Tangier.

Today it would see the magnificent waterfall of Pulai.

We drove down a narrow dirt path off the highway, through thick jungle that had been cut away enough to reveal a small parking area at the end scattered with haphazard cars. Like every day in Malaysia, we sweltered in the stifling equator sun as we exited the cool air-conditioned car. The hiking path itself was well paved, covered with large trees, overgrown vines, and dark green foliage that provided some respite from the heat. Wide as a road and as steep as it could be, the path twisted and turned for miles. No one on the path spoke English, locals only. We were the outliers.

Brett and I were competitive to a fault. Early in our relationship we would get in rip-roaring fights while playing gin. Our competitiveness with ourselves and each other pushed us to do as much as we could, as fast as we could. Today was no different.

We had a silent understanding: neither of us would give up. We each wore our headphones and listened to music as we attacked the climb. Strong beats and powerful lyrics encouraged us to keep going. We took turns pushing the stroller, fifty pounds of a three-year-old Kyla and all of our crap, one song at a time. The ascent was so steep that the stroller was over our heads for most of the climb. We stopped at certain points to catch our breath, listen to the hidden waterfall, and let Kyla run around for a minute, encouraging her to climb with us. Every time we passed the locals casually walking down the mountain, they would look at us with strange and confused stares, in awe of our stupidity.

We were drenched with sweat, out of breath, and feeling accomplished as we neared the summit. After hours of constant, steady climbing in the seemingly 110-degree steam room of Pulai, we turned the last corner, anticipating the most beautiful waterfall. Instead, painted in large, white letters was the word "STOP." Beyond the road was a high electric fence, defending what looked like a restricted area full of cell towers.

*What the fuck?* I thought. "You've got to be kidding me. Are they serious?! Where's the waterfall?" I threw up my hands, asking the question to no one.

"Seriously, Stace, you don't know?!" he jeered.

"Well, I assumed it was at the top," I retorted.

"Huh," he contemplated, attempting to minimize my anger.

"Well, at least we made it to this wonderful stop sign." I sarcastically searched for a silver lining. All that effort and no reward. I was pissed.

Brett, in his typical "oh well" fashion, shrugged it off with a smile and turned around to descend the mountain.

Halfway down, he began to rub the right side of his abdomen near his ribcage. Never complaining about pain, he briefly mentioned he thought maybe he pulled something. The decline was so steep that it took us over two hours to climb and only forty-five minutes to get down. Ironically, we discovered the entrance to the waterfall at the bottom, which was only a few minutes into the start of the hike. I had promised Kyla time in the water, which was her favorite place to play, so we took off our shoes and briefly dipped our toes in the trickling creek that ran down the mountain. Brett didn't. He was ready to go and encouraged us to leave.

Driving back home toward Johor Bahru, he casually mentioned again, "My side doesn't feel great. I think I might keep driving to Singapore and go to urgent care."

Intuitively, he must have known. He hated hospitals. He would never choose to go to one unless something was really wrong. Even when things were really wrong, he had refused to go in the past. Now he was volunteering. Something didn't add up.

*What is he not telling me?* I wondered. But I responded, "Okay, sure, let's go."

X-rays revealed a possible hairline fracture in his ribs, though he had experienced no trauma. The ER doctor seemed confused and walked us over to the orthopedic surgeon down the hall. The surgeon spent an hour with Brett, getting to know him, reviewing his medical history, and analyzing the images. I entertained Kyla outside in the hall as she ran back and forth, full of energy and joy.

"I don't see any fractures," the surgeon said. "To be honest, with your family history of cancer and your great medical insurance as an expat, you might as well run some more tests to rule out anything. If you want, we can do an MRI and a CT scan, just to be sure nothing is wrong."

Brett agreed.

He ran all the tests, and we left waiting for results. The phone call came just as we arrived home an hour later.

"You need to come back tomorrow," the doctor advised.

"Okay...?"

I watched as Brett sat and listened to an explanation, his poker face revealing nothing. He hung up the phone and was silent. I waited patiently, hoping for good news.

"I need to go back tomorrow in the morning…it's not good."

"Okay, do you want me to go with you?" I asked.

"Yes. Let's figure out who to leave Kyla with. Maybe Andrea."

"Okay."

"And pack a bag," he said.

Our fast-paced life had come to a screeching halt. "STOP," the sign read.

It was January 2015. Brett was thirty-five.

# Bears Fuck Shit Up

Smartphones, Brett, and I had a contentious relationship. He and his phone were codependent lovers, always near each other, waiting for the other to reach out and need something. I often felt like I was the third wheel in the story, waiting on the sidelines for him to stop the deep connection he had with the phone, disengage with the person he was talking to, and pay attention to me. I secretly wished they would break up and said more than once over dinner during date night that he and his phone needed to get a room. It was so inappropriate to show so much affection for each other in public.

On the other hand, his phone was his superpower. Brett's reliability to answer his phone at any hour of the day made him a loyal friend and an accountable employee in the shipping industry. His friends received phone calls from him all the time. He would always ask them about themselves first: "How are you? What's going on?" His big heart, listening ear, and jovial nature solidified friendships with many people he encountered. He and his phone sustained those friendships.

His nickname was "The Vault" during his career with APM Terminals, because anywhere he worked, people trusted him with their secrets. They relied on him to answer his phone, listen, and help solve any problem that arose. His ability to put out fires was effective and efficient, and he usually did it through his phone. He was always on call and always willing to help.

I ignored most of the things he did on his phone out of sheer frustration and selective attention. He had desensitized me over the years. But when we got the call from Singapore after our stop-sign hike, he knew I was going to need support. He picked up his phone and secretly reached out to our crew of friends back home in the United States. Most of them had competed for Cal as student-athletes: rowers, swimmers, and water polo players. All of them had a wonderfully fucked-up sense of humor. The running group message with them was titled Bears Fuck Shit Up (BFSU), a mantra that we used throughout Brett's fight with cancer to stay positive and keep charging. It reminded us of all the hard work and adversity we had overcome as Bears together and that we were capable of anything.

He initially started the group message with them without me:

B: Hey! How are you guys?

BFSU: Good
great
livin' the dream
working

B: Good to hear. Just wanted to give you all a heads up...Going into emergency surgery tomorrow, might not come out of it. Stace needs help. Don't tell her I said anything.

BFSU: got it
ok
on it
sure
10-4

B: thanks

BFSU: anything for you B
what's the surgery for?

B: Oh, just a tumor in my ass. Been blowing diarrhea and blood out my butt for a while. Thought it was bad food and hemorrhoids. Guess not, haha!

BFSU:   Well go take care of that shit!
               Seriously, baby wipes dude, all day.
               you know that anal sex will kill ya!

B:  It's experimenting up to 13 times. Haha

BFSU:   Keep telling yourself that.

B:  Will do, thanks. Good night fuckers!

BFSU:   good luck tomorrow
               go fuck that shit up
               night fucker!

When Brett and I arrived at the private hospital in Singapore the morning after the Pulai hike, the orthopedic doctor met with us to review the PET scan in detail. My good friend D, who was the wife of one of Brett's friends, was living in Singapore and came to the hospital to check on me. As I sat next to her on a waiting room bench, she handed me a bag with a few pills in it.

"Here, take two right now," she said.

"What's this?"

"Xanax. You're going to need it."

"But I don't like taking pills," I said. "I'm scared. The only thing I've ever taken was Percocet when Kyla was born for my C-section pain. That was gnarly."

"Look, I get it, honey." Her southern accent and charm soothed me. "But here's the deal. You need something to take the edge off. These are mild, and they help with anxiety. If there's *any* time to consider taking this, honey, it's right now." She dealt with anxiety and understood the magic of Xanax.

"Okay, thank you."

I entered the doctor's office ready to hear the details. Brett and I sat side by side, holding our breath, and waited for the doctor to speak.

"You have Stage IV colon cancer." The weight of this statement landed deep in the pit of my stomach. "There's a large primary tumor in your colon, the para-aortic lymph nodes have been affected up the chain toward your abdomen, and there are small cancerous masses all over your liver. I want you to meet my good friend, Dr. Chan, who is the best GI doctor in the country. He will give you more details about the next steps."

The customer service in this private hospital was remarkably different from the United States system of healthcare. Their concern for the patient and close proximity expedited the process to save Brett's life. The orthopedic surgeon walked us over to meet Dr. Chan down the hall. They had a great rapport and wanted us to feel as comfortable as possible. They planned to do surgery, but first Dr. Chan wanted to take a look at Brett's insides with a scope and get the lay of the land. Dr. Chan was an expert at performing colonoscopies and surgeries for the intestines. He prepped Brett for the exam, not knowing the extent of the issue.

"I guess we're going to be pretty close when this is over, Doc. I don't even let my wife get near the places you're going to explore," Brett teased him, trying to make light of the situation.

"Yes, well, I have a lot of experience. I haven't had any complaints."

"That's because all your patients are sedated."

"*Touché.*" He handed Brett the colon cleanse. "Don't worry—we'll take care of you. Drink up."

"Nice foreplay, Doc!"

"Anytime." He winked, said, "See you soon," and walked out of the room.

For the next four hours, Brett and the toilet were best friends. He wore a loose hospital gown, open in the back for quick access to empty his system. The magic juice cleared him out from top to bottom. After the colonoscopy, Brett was admitted for emergency surgery the same day. "Unfortunately, I wasn't able to get the scope inside the colon because of the size of the tumor. The restriction made the colon passageway about the size of the tip of a pencil. Frankly, I have no idea how you've been able to go to the bathroom," Dr. Chan debriefed us.

"It's been a challenge," Brett admitted.

"That's understandable," the doctor empathized.

"I thought he was just playing games on his phone in there," I joked.

"Well, we're going to have to get that tumor out of there now."

Resection of the colon is a complex process when there is cancer. It's important to remove the primary tumor and as many of the secondary masses as possible, without spreading the cancer into the bloodstream. The surgeon cuts a pizza slice out of the colon where all the cancer is and then sews it back up.

I gave Brett a kiss as he was wheeled into surgery. "I love you. You got this!" I reassured him.

He squeezed my hand and kissed it, saying, "I love you too."

Six hours later, trying to pass the time, I read every single thing I could on colon cancer. I studied every new vocabulary word that the doctors had said from the initial scans and diagnosis. If we were going to be prepared, I needed to educate myself, learn a new language, and ask all the right questions. More time passed, and I waited, hoping Brett was alright. I sat in the dark, heavily air-conditioned waiting room and finally decided to call a few close family members who would be starting their day in the United States. I didn't want to call. That would make it real. But I knew I had to tell his mom and my parents. In shock, the conversations were short and muddled. When there was nothing left to do, I sat and prayed. And the time passed...

The doctor called me to tell me the news when Brett was in recovery. "I was able to remove the primary tumor completely, as well as nineteen lymph nodes that were affected. We will biopsy the cancerous tissue to identify the most successful treatment plan. He'll need chemotherapy and possibly radiation for his liver. There are too many masses, and they are too small to remove. He would have no liver tissue left. He's doing well and should be moved to a room soon. I'll have the nurses come get you when he is transferred from recovery."

"Thank you. Thank you for everything," I quietly expressed my exhaustion and gratitude.

"You're welcome. I did everything I could to give him the best fighting chance at this. But he's got a long road ahead."

The next day, Brett teased the petite Asian nurses as he walked around the hospital bed to get out of the way so they could change the sheets. "Do you like my new tail? Wanna pet it?" he asked, referring to the tube out his rear end, one of the many tubes protruding from his body to drain off the fluids from surgery.

They bashfully looked down and giggled. They had never experienced such a large, ridiculous man before with such a twisted sense of humor. His hospital bed looked like it was made for a small child with his six-foot-five frame in it. They had to stack blankets and pillows on the ground at the end of the bed so the bottom half of his legs would have some place to rest. It provided the comic relief we all needed.

My phone began blowing up with messages from the BFSU crew. They had started a new group message with all of us on it and were sending joke after joke. The jokes didn't stop for two years. Every day, starting the morning after surgery in the hospital, there was a running litany of perverted jokes and sharing of humorous daily activities to get us through the hard times. We were processing the information as a team, trying to overcome the challenge together. They even renamed the group with emojis that represented Bears Fuck Shit Up. Later, one of our friends made silicone bracelets with the emojis on the outside and "fuck cancer" on the inside, and distributed them to all our family and friends. Teammates for life. They surrounded us with love and strength. Brett wore his bracelet for all two years of his fight, a rallying cry to remind him: "Bears Fuck Shit Up!"

# The Fight

## January 2015, Age 33

When Brett was diagnosed with Stage IV colon cancer at age thirty-five, he was given an expiration date: January 2017. "Two years," the doctor simply stated, citing the statistical timeline of survival.

And boy did we make those two years count. We fought as hard as we lived. We were competitors who knew how to work hard for a goal. We would beat the odds with everything they threw at us. As a team, we cultivated an extensive network of support: doctors, nurses, family, friends, others fighting, and survivors who embodied the desire to win. Winning meant more life.

What does it mean to live? Brett's definition was to thrive in the time he had left. *Tomorrow is not guaranteed, so make today count.* He made healthy choices, communed with others, volunteered his time coaching, connected with God, and did as much as he could to serve, to inspire, and to fight until his body decided to die.

## September 2015, Age 34

"Go! Go! Go!"

Three hundred and seventy-five people jumped off the large ferry into the San Francisco Bay. The dark, brown, murky water was absolutely freezing. I screamed with joy and fear as adrenaline and the previous night's alcohol consumption coursed through my veins. It was a common rite of passage for Swim Across America rookies in our Olympian group to drink their tails off the night before their first charity swim. And if you could read the makeup of my blood like an ingredient label it would read, from greatest to least concentration: alcohol, adrenaline, and hot boat coffee mixed with plasma and red blood cells. This imbalanced yet perfect combination energized me, kept me warm, and helped me relax as I faced one of my biggest fears. I stopped, took my goggles off, and looked up at the magnificent brick-red Golden Gate Bridge. I was floating beneath it in the middle of the bay, swimming with the sharks.

Forty-eight hours earlier, I'd been sitting on a plane from Malaysia to SFO, journaling through tears about my fear of losing Brett. I could only truly process my grief when I was alone and free to feel without affecting others. I was on the plane because our good friend Heather Petri had convinced Brett and me that I should participate in Swim Across America, San Francisco (SAA, SF). She was in charge of recruiting and organizing the Olympians who wanted to participate in the swim to raise funds and awareness for cancer research locally. The community that is involved in SAA, SF is inspirational and well connected in the cancer research network. I was petrified of swimming in the bay, but her forethought about the possible future benefits for both Brett and me, along with her never-ending enthusiasm, pushed me to do it. She knew I needed something positive to help make a difference in Brett's fight and keep our spirits up.

At the time of my first SAA, SF swim in late September of 2015, Brett had been doing chemo treatments for eight months. When we first moved back to Southern California, Brett's work had given him a six-month paid sabbatical, which enabled him to truly focus on the fight without the stress of work. This was an absolute miracle. The husband I always wanted, who didn't prioritize work over his family, appeared. He focused on the protocol to live and spent every possible moment with us while he still could. He lived for every day, and it was inspiring—the only true gift of cancer. We appreciated every day, no matter the circumstances, and he fought back the gremlins that churned inside him from the chemo. His goal was to beat the cancer and return to work in Malaysia after the six months ended.

After six months of aggressive treatment, twelve rounds of chemo (one every other week without breaks), his cancer markers had fallen significantly, which meant the cancer was inactive and the chemotherapy was working. Brett pushed to return to Malaysia. My intuition pushed back. I was so apprehensive, because I associated Malaysia with his demise.

"It will either make me or kill me," he had foreshadowed when we left Morocco. We'd been living in Tangier for two years for Brett's first overseas job with APM Terminals when the Port of Tanjung Pelepas in Malaysia recruited him to work the much larger APM terminal: sixty cranes versus twelve. I didn't want to go, because we had a good thing going in Tangier as a family. We lived across from the beach on the Strait of Gibraltar in a beautiful home with a pool. We watched the sun every night dip below the horizon into the Mediterranean Sea, and I enjoyed staying home with Kyla and working part-time teaching yoga. But that all changed when we moved to Malaysia. Work never stopped for him, and I thought the stress was killing him.

After the six-month sabbatical and seemingly effective cancer treatment protocol, Brett was ready to go back to work in Malaysia. I didn't want to go back, and my body was telling me that we shouldn't.

My sister helped me make the decision. "You have stood by his side through this whole fight, taken him to every doctor's appointment, read about every possible treatment option and cancer research," she said. "*And* he's doing better. You are almost done with this fight! Now is NOT the time to give up! You have to keep supporting him. You have to go. He's going to go with or without you. But he needs you still. You will regret it if he goes alone."

"But what if I have the worst feeling about going? I don't think we should. I'm scared it's going to kill him," I confessed through tears.

"I think you need to support him. Maybe you should look into taking an antidepressant or something for anxiety. You are dealing with a lot. Maybe that would help. Just consider it," Lish gently urged, because she knew I hated being told what to do. I was stubborn.

"Ugh! Maybe. I know you're right that I should support him, but I still don't want to go." I rubbed my eyes raw from stress and fatigue. They burned from the tears and all my conflicted emotions. Later that week, I filled my prescriptions for Lexapro and Xanax. Then I got on the plane with Brett and Kyla and flew back to Malaysia, suppressing the fearfully dark premonitions.

When we returned to JB (Johor Bahru, Malaysia), Brett walked through the door of his work on the first day with his arms up victoriously, larger than life, declaring, "I'm back!" He celebrated with his coworkers, showing triumph through his actions and appearance. He hadn't lost any hair, and his weight had stabilized. No one would have known he was a cancer patient. He'd set a goal to return, and he achieved it. I was happy for him because he was so happy. But after seven weeks in Malaysia and three more chemo treatments, the cancer markers started to move in the wrong direction. The cancer was becoming more active again. I was overwhelmed. My fears were coming true. I prayed hard for a solution.

In the meantime, I had already committed to going to the charity swim in San Francisco. Brett knew I needed a break and pushed me to go have fun. Although things seemed so uncertain, I was relieved to get a reprieve from the supportive role as stay-at-home mom and wife/health advocate for Brett. I thought the trip would give me some time to process everything and refill my emotional bucket.

I arrived in San Francisco on a Friday and met a few friends in the city for dinner. While eating the appetizers, I received the news that no mom wants to hear. I got a call from Andrea, our loving Australian expat neighbor who had become part of our expat family. Living overseas, you quickly make friends with other expats to develop a support system far away from home. Andrea was taking care of Kyla for the weekend while Brett was getting chemo across the bridge in Singapore.

"So, don't freak out," Andrea warned over the phone. "She's fine, but we think Kyla broke her arm."

"What?!...How?"

"We took the kids to the Angry Birds park in the mall, and she was swinging on a rope above the ball pit. Her arm twisted the wrong way, and we think she broke it," Andrea explained. "She wouldn't stop screaming all the way to the hospital in JB. The doctor said it wasn't broken, but I think we're going to drive her to Singapore for a second opinion."

"I think that's a good idea. Does Brett know? He's in Singapore right now getting treatment."

"Yes, we called him, and he suggested we bring her there. There's a children's hospital we can take her to. I'm going to stop by your house now and grab her passport."

"Okay. Ugh...I'm so sorry I'm not there. Can I talk to her?"

"She's unavailable right now, actually," she laughed, trying to find humor in the situation. "She screamed until she passed out, so right now she's asleep on Sam's lap."

"Okay, don't wake her up. Just please keep me posted."

"Will do."

Andrea and her family drove our scared, exhausted four-year-old daughter to Singapore to get X-rays and a cast. Brett met them at the children's hospital, but he couldn't go in to be with her because of his compromised immune system. Instead, he sat outside and waited for her to get her cast on. I felt so helpless, thousands of miles away and unable to be there for either of them.

"How are you feeling?" I asked him over the phone as he waited in the sweltering midday equator heat and I sat outside the restaurant in the cold San Francisco night air. We were complete opposites in location, time, and climate.

"I'm fine," he answered, compartmentalizing his own pain and the paternal pain he felt for our child.

"I feel terrible neither of us are there for her," I admitted.

"Don't worry, Andrea's got her. She'll be okay."

"Okay, I love you. Please call me when she's done."

"Yup." He never complained, but I could hear his frustration in his one-word response.

Later that night, Andrea reassured me over the phone, "Don't worry, your baby's fine. She was so brave, and she's fast asleep on Sam's lap again. We're driving back to

JB now. Brett's doing okay too. Finished his chemo like a champ! Now go swim, girl! You got this!"

"Thank you, Andrea."

My second night in San Francisco, Saturday, was the "you're the rookie, so let's see how fucked up you can get and still be able to swim tomorrow" challenge. Luckily, thanks to the Mermaid Mafia crew (women I'd bonded with through the Olympics and other swim adventures), I passed with flying colors. I attribute my success to our student-athlete "train hard, party hard" mentality, which prepared us to survive nights of binge drinking by consuming copious amounts of greasy, late-night food and rehydrating with our sports water bottles. I wanted to let loose. After eight months of no drinking, no sugar, no meat, and following a no-temptation regime to win the concerted effort to keep Brett alive, I was ready to not give a fuck!

Late into the night, the crew, who knew how to take care of each other, decided I needed something in my stomach to recover from pulling the trigger to throw up the excess alcohol I had ingested but not digested yet. Heather, being the responsible one, drove us back to Berkeley from a beach in the city and ordered the infamous Berkeley trifecta that brought us all back to life: a Kingpin donut (only when it is "hot, fresh, now"), a La Burrita burrito, and a Top Dog hot dog—delicious 2:00 a.m. drunk food on Durant Avenue.

After a few hours of sleep, with very full stomachs, we woke up and jumped in a shuttle at 5:00 a.m. to get from the hotel to the staging area for the swim. Still drunk and silly from all the shenanigans, we laughed all the way to Little Marina Green. We loaded onto a famous San Fran red trolley and sang to the radio as we rode through the dark, empty streets of the city past Pier 39 where the ferry boat launched, carrying all 375 passengers.

On the boat, cruising in the bay before everyone jumped off, there was a magical hour of camaraderie mixed with nervousness and love. Bagels and hot coffee soothed anxious stomachs and awakened sleepy brains. Each participant chose a fake tattoo to mark their body, commemorating the person(s) for whom they were swimming. We gathered on the floor of the main deck and listened to stories that answered the Swim Across America question, "Why do we swim?" We laughed and cried together, bonded by the terrible disease that affected us all.

Then, we selected a gerbera daisy from the flower-filled fifteen-gallon buckets all over the deck. We each had a private moment to say a prayer and throw our chosen flower into the water to honor the people in our lives who were fighting or had passed on. I stood there at the back of the boat and cried, alone. Fear drained from my eyes. I squeezed them shut and prayed, *Please, God, give Brett the strength to fight this disease. Please give me the strength to support him and enjoy each moment together without fear. Please let him be here next year.*

As I threw my magenta gerbera daisy into the water, the CEO of Swim Across America, Janelle, wrapped her arm around my shoulder and pulled me close. "He will be here next year," she quietly whispered, unknowingly repeating my silent prayer.

I started to shudder with sadness, acknowledging the sameness of her words to my thoughts. Tears flowed down my face, and she held me closer with a squeeze. The sunshine peeked through a break in the clouds, and two dolphins emerged near the boat. I believe in signs, and this moment imprinted in my brain the power of prayer and love. *He will be here next year*, I silently repeated to myself, secretly hoping I could will it to happen.

"Thank you," I said to Janelle. "I hope so." I smiled and squeezed her back.

Shortly after this moment, all 375 participants jumped off the ferry and I found myself floating under the Golden Gate, supported by the great expanse of dark water below me, in awe of the bridge's grandeur and my place beneath it. Magically, the magenta flower that I had thrown off the boat to pray for Brett's fight floated back to me with the incoming flood of water. Overwhelmed with emotion, I was astounded that in the greatness of the bay, my single flower could reappear in my path. I reached out, grabbed it, held it up, and yelled with joy, leaping out of the water, as Kristy took a picture to capture the surrealness of the moment. I was hooked. I knew why I swam. And I knew I would swim again.

The singular focus that you need to make an Olympic team in an individual sport like swimming, and the same laser focus you need to win the seemingly impossible battle to fight Stage IV colon cancer, increases the possibility of missing things happening around you. The effect amplifies when you combine this tunnel vision with the gray, fuzzy cloud of grief, when senses are blurred and memory is muted. I learned in the two years of Brett's battle with cancer that people experience grief long before their loved one dies, when the daily anticipation of death exists. Each day your loved one loses the ability to do something, you grieve. You grieve the loss of future events. You grieve the loss of the plans you've made, which will be broken again and again.

The following year, 2016, after my first experience with Swim Across America, I signed up to do the event in San Francisco again. Now that I understood the impact I could have on the future survival rate for a cancer diagnosis, I wanted to raise as much money as possible. I recruited anyone who wanted to swim with me to ultimately raise funds for the cause. Brett's company, AP Møller – Mærsk, made a large donation as well, and Brett and I planned the trip to celebrate the event together. We would go as a family. I wanted Brett and Kyla to experience the power, the energy, and the goodness of the SAA community and the cause. Brett took a week off from his chemo routine so he would feel his best and be up for the trip. It would be our last adventure weekend as a family.

We stayed at the beautiful, historic Claremont Hotel in Berkeley with the Mermaids, including Heather, Rada, Kristy, and Monkey. We played in the gorgeous hotel pool with Kyla and explored the grounds like we always did as a family on our travel adventures.

On Friday, I participated in the hospital visits that Swim Across America and Heather arranged for the Olympians to have the privilege of meeting and connecting with kids who were fighting hard battles with cancer. We also connected with the doctors who received the funds from the swim, Dr. Rob Goldsby and Dr. Julie Saba, who were dedicating their lives to support the children and research new ways to fight this deadly disease. The kids in the hospital signed our swim caps so that we could support them during our swim in the bay.

"Look out there tomorrow," we shared with them as we pointed to the large expanse of water outside the hospital windows, "and you'll see us swimming for you." This inevitably always created a smile on the child's face.

Heather recounted the weekend with me from her perspective:

> When you guys were here for that swim and we were able to house you at the Claremont for the weekend, I began to notice the verbiage of Brett's narratives, and his conversations with me were in the future tense. In a time where he would no longer be with us.
>
> I had always loved that throughout his fight and my correspondences with him via text or in person you could feel his passion for championing this disease. For you, for Kyla, for the sheer competitive nature of not letting cancer win. (Ever the athlete mindset, no?!)
>
> But that weekend was markedly different. I listened and took in what that meant to me, for him, and for your family.
>
> So, by the time we had landed at the Claremont Hotel bar, I was reveling in the joy I was witnessing between all of us as friends. There was a freedom in all your drunkenness and the positive spirit that drew us all together. It was Brett. We always connect to fight cancer, but that year we were fighting tooth and nail alongside him.
>
> He brought us all shots to commemorate this time between us all. I, being the crew's "wrangler" for the

weekend, balked at taking it. He looked me straight in the eye and said, "No. This moment is important to celebrate." Of course, I was ever a team player and knew he was right. We all grabbed our shots and toasted the moment. I can't remember what words were said at that particular moment because I was just enjoying that we were together.

He was sitting on my left at the end of the table. You, Kristy, and Monkey were joyously talking about something standing together to our right. He reached over and grabbed my wrist that lay on the table. He said to me, "I need you to continue to be there for Stace." He continued to reiterate a few things we had talked about on occasion before. About how there would be a few people he was certain would be able to understand what she needed, and that true deep friendship was what was important. He felt I would be important to this inner circle. I was honored. I already felt deeply connected to you guys for all our past parallel experiences and instinctively knew what he was talking about, but had never had a conversation so pointedly regarding the absolute certainty of future friendship.

You all kept drinking the night away and it was a joy to watch. To have the ability to soak up that time all the while knowing that very soon, we would not be able to recreate it.

Brett knew Heather and I needed each other. He knew when he passed, a new relationship would need to take over his role and ability to uplift me and celebrate my uniqueness. I am so grateful that he saw this golden connection between Heather and me and made a point of empowering Heather to sustain it. Her clarity in that moment was impactful to me then, and it still is. Our friendship continues to help us through life, and Brett's spirit lives on through his call to action.

# Messages

Communication can be profound and unique. Sometimes someone speaks a message to you that is so simple and timely, it's easy to feel like it comes from something bigger than anything we can explain. Words can flow through us to each other and be so impactful that we are taken aback, and the memory is imprinted on our hearts.

I experienced such foreshadowing of a distant future.

More than once, I felt this message from above through journaling and from different people during the two years of Brett's intense battle with cancer. Serendipitous events have a miraculous way of relaying these messages when you need to hear them the most.

## September 2016, Age 35

At the pivotal downturn of Brett's health (although we didn't know that's what it was at the time), I went to support my childhood friend who was getting married in a beautiful, renovated barn in a suburban area of Ohio. She asked me to be a bridesmaid, and of course, I agreed, despite the hardship and uncertainty I was experiencing at home.

Brett encouraged me to go have fun while he arranged a trip to Rancho La Quinta, California, with Kyla to spend time with his godparents, Michele and Randy. He and Kyla enjoyed a "daddy-daughter weekend" in the warm desert air with golf-cart adventures and family pool time. Knowing they needed this time with each other to play in Brett's favorite playground, I was grateful to take a break from my role at home. I knew the solo trip to Ohio would give me time to clear my head.

Airplanes always create space for me to reflect. Flying over the Earth's surface, thirty thousand feet in the air, I often feel a sense of clarity regarding the problems I'm experiencing on the ground. Passing over the majesty of the Grand Canyon, I couldn't help but imagine it as a metaphor for the contrasting feelings I was experiencing. Its eternal and expansive beauty represented the joyful celebration of a wedding: the hopeful future of two people, together forever. Its deep chasms caused by prehistoric erosion and relentless moving water represented the change and division of all things over time.

Unfortunately, you can't stop the current of life. You can learn to swim—and choose to swim with it or against it.

I had hoped to float on top of it, like a lazy river, basking in the glow of sunlight and never-ending love. But life isn't always a lazy river. Sometimes, around the bend, are tumultuous rapids. I was grieving the uncertainty of my forever future with Brett, hearing the roar of a magnificent and life-threatening waterfall in the distance.

Away from my family, in a plane full of strangers, I could let down my guard and remove the "mask of strength" that hid my true feelings from everyone, including myself. I felt the need to journal on the three-hour flight, while my tears stained the ink:

> *September 23, 2016*
> *Twenty months...so much has happened and yet I feel like the day Brett was diagnosed. Scared of his death. Why am I scared of his death?*
> > *I will miss my best friend.*
> > *I won't have a father for Kyla.*
> > *I won't be able to share everything with him anymore.*
> > *A piece of me will be gone.*
> > *I don't know how to live my life without him.*
> > *I am physically sick when I think about it.*
> > *Never experienced this kind of loss.*
> *I'm afraid to have to deal with the consequences of his death:*
> > *People surrounding me.*

*Finances—will we lose our house?*

*Can I support Kyla by myself?*

*How do I grieve?*

*How do I talk to Kyla about death?*

*How do I prepare?*

*Will I regret the time I have left with him?*

*What are the steps I have to take to prepare?*

*Support group—Who will understand?*

*Who has the answers?*

*Finances—secure a job*

*Simplify expenses*

*Roommate?*

*Refinance house*

*What will happen to my constitution?*

*How will I cope?*

*Will I lose my faith?*

*Will I be angry, sad, lost, depressed?*

*How will I still be a good mom and deal with Kyla?*

*What are my resources?*

*Who will my support system be?*

*What will my life look like without him?*

*I can do it. I am strong, independent, motivated, determined, optimistic.*

*Other people have done it and are ok.*

*How do I show Brett I can do it?*

*Help him go peacefully. I have to talk to him. I have to tell him my beliefs.*

*I have to tell him how much I love him and that I will be ok.*
*I will stay strong for Kyla.*
*I believe he will watch over us.*
*I believe he will be in Heaven.*
*He will live on through Kyla.*
*What do I need from him before he goes?*
*His wishes for Kyla.*
*His wishes for his funeral, burial, etc.*
*His wishes for me.*
*Recordings of his voice.*
*Videos of him with Kyla.*
*Books for Kyla.*
*What to do with all his stuff…?*

*I need to write a letter to Brett to tell him how I feel before he gets too sick.*
*I need to write him a contract for death…*

And through this journaling I was grateful for the clarity of the final message received. Unknowingly, the voice in my head and my pen switched from first to third person, and it was commanding me:

You married Brett because he was your best friend, not because you were afraid to be alone. So, don't be afraid now. You will survive. You will Rise up! You will

miss him; he will always be with you. Keep him close
to your heart. You can do this!

This command gave me the strength to continue to write,
and what came out next was a contract for death from me to
Brett—and ultimately for myself:

*I promise to stay strong for Kyla.*
*I promise to laugh and be silly, dance, and play happy
music.*
*I promise to raise her to be a strong, loving, smart
independent woman.*
*I promise to discipline Kyla and support her as she grows.*
*I promise to hold Kyla to your standards:*
  *1. Don't lie*
  *2. Respectful: Yes ma'am, Please, Thank you.*
  *3. Commitment, loyalty, servant to God.*
*I promise to love Kyla for both of us and tell her every
day.*
*I promise to protect Kyla.*
*I promise to talk about you with Kyla.*
*I promise to work hard to keep our house, be debt free.*
*I will honor your memory.*
*I promise I will process your death in a positive healing
way: exercise, support groups, bible study, church
involvement, serve others, journaling.*
*I promise to FLOURISH. I will make our lives work
even without you there.*

*I promise to take care of myself, make the right choices.*
*I won't give into grief. I won't lose my Faith.*
*I won't self-destruct. I won't forget. I won't shut down. I*
*will ask for help.*
*I won't stop. I will rise up. I will pray.*
*I will see you in Heaven.*

In Ohio at the wedding reception, a woman came up to me, full of life and energy. She radiated so much joy as I watched her dance, light and carefree. My friend's mom, the mother of the bride, had told this woman about my struggles with Brett's fight against cancer, and she had caught me in a moment of internal sadness. She sat down next to me to share a message with a giant smile on her face: "When I was your age, the love of my life, my first husband, passed away. It was awful, and I thought I would never feel joy again. But I got through it, and so will you." She gave me a huge hug, and I felt all of her strength. She wasn't making it up, and her words stuck with me, although they seemed hard to believe.

## November 2016, Age 35

After forty rounds of chemo (one round every other week), injected radiation to his liver, external radiation to his chest, and Gamma Knife radiation to his brain, Brett's last ten weeks of life were absolute torture. I internally felt like I had entered the seventh circle of hell, but we were truly only waiting, stuck in Dante's purgatory. Brett developed ascites and needed draining every four days, or his abdomen would fill with fluid like a balloon. He was not able to keep food down anymore, which confirmed what we didn't say out loud. This was the beginning of the end.

Desperate for him to live, we tried a Hail Mary. Directly after an ascites drainage, we drove down to San Diego for an experimental immunotherapy treatment I had found while scouring the internet in the aisle of an Albertsons grocery store for any new research or clinical trials. Every moment, the logistics of his fight were running through my thoughts, no matter where I was or what I was doing in the daily monotony of life—even when buying groceries. The potential plans to survive flowed through my mind as fast as a cheetah sprinting, but for the distance of an ultramarathon. Needless to say, we both were exhausted. However, we didn't let it stop us from searching for answers to a problem we ultimately couldn't fix.

Brett had to pass all the bloodwork and interview to be accepted into the clinical trial. Desperation causes a man to do things he normally wouldn't do, and Brett, who never lied, was willing to do anything to live. He lied through his teeth to hide the ascites that had taken over his body. But his body couldn't lie. His bloodwork came back too low on sodium, and he was prescribed an ungodly number of sodium tablets in an attempt to reach homoeostasis and qualify him for the clinical trial.

Disheartened yet still hopeful, we sat together in the hotel that night while he shoved one juicy bite of a sumptuous Marriott burger into his mouth. He prayed hard that it would stay down and nourish his empty, dying body. But it didn't. He knew, and I knew—yet we still forged on, hoping for a miracle. His body ultimately was rejecting everything. It was full of poison and couldn't sustain the physiological mechanisms of life.

The next night, I found him face down on the corner of the bed, legs sprawled with one foot on the floor, unresponsive. As I rubbed his back lightly to see if he was sleeping, he started to mumble gibberish. He suffered a ministroke that affected his speech and mobility. We took him into urgent care, where they filled his body with fluids (that ironically would go directly to his abdominal cavity, because his kidneys were kaput). The hydration helped the color return to his face, he regained the ability to walk and speak, and we hoped he would get good news that he could join the trial. But the good news never came.

# Stolen Dance

## December 2016, Age 35

The night before my husband died, I found myself finally alone with him, and I had to dance. Holding his hand, attached to his comatose body, I needed him to know I was going to be okay. I was going to dance around him, celebrating our life and our forever love together. Led by my heart, not my head, I felt the warm joy of our marriage flow through me and into him. I listened to the lyrics of the song, "Stolen Dance" by Milky Chance, and they too closely resembled the moment, like the song was about us:

"I want you by my side, so that I never have to be alone..."[34]

The tears streamed down my face.

"I hope they didn't get your mind, your heart is too strong anyway..."[35]

His heart continued to beat, but his communication had ceased. I knew his mind was still there, listening. More tears filled my eyes, and my chest constricted. I knew I had to fight the overwhelming feeling of grief, so I kept dancing through the tears. I wanted him to feel joy, peace, and love as his soul left his body. A stolen dance...on borrowed time.

The previous eight days had been a whirlwind. He had decided that his fight was over. He was the "Big Dog" as his doctor and close family friend, Docman, called him. He seemed to have a superhuman ability to compartmentalize pain and sustain the most aggressive and toxic protocol to fight Stage IV colon cancer.

We drove over the 73 Toll Road to Hoag Hospital—and both knew he wouldn't be coming back home. My heart throbbed and my stomach ached as it digested the fear, sadness, disappointment, and rage deep down inside me. I tightly held static tension in my psoas muscle, an animalistic instinctual protection from external danger. But the danger wasn't external. There was nothing to fight. Cancer is a hidden, secretive, destructive disease that does not discriminate.

The danger was deep inside us both, consuming his body and creating a tornado in my brain, which spun with unanswered questions: *Will I be able to process this grief? Can I live without the love of my life, my best friend? Will I ever see him again? How will I raise Kyla without her dad? How will I breathe?* Determined not to let one drop of emotion affect my dying husband, my white knuckles gripped the steering wheel and my dark eyes filled with tears. I swallowed all the questions and doubts. I was driving him to his death. As I drove, I asked him to record short messages on our phone to Kyla. I knew she and I would need to hear his voice when he was gone.

We checked into the palliative care unit and were greeted by friendly nurses and solemn, pragmatic doctors. Brett shared with the care team that he would not eat or drink anything anymore. He wanted to let his body go to heaven riding the morphine train.

The moment he pushed the morphine button connected to an IV in the semipermanent subcutaneous port under his left collarbone, I had my husband back. It struck me how much pain he had truly been in. He had been a shell of a human for ten weeks, silently pushing through indescribable pain with strong opioids, steroids, Adderall, and other drugs to keep him going while the chemo and cancer poisoned his body and shut down his organs. Human brains aren't able to sustain any coherent train of thought or verbalize it well when this specific cocktail of drugs enters the bloodstream. We often laughed at his "chemo brain," slow response time, and distant stare. But in the hospital, under palliative care, with only morphine flowing through him like the sweet nectar of life, he was able to smile, talk, tease, and laugh for the first time in a long time—and for the last time of his life.

Every person close to us came to visit. There was a revolving door of people coming to say goodbye, creating a blur of emotions and people. The silver lining of cancer is you have time to say goodbye, make plans, and live each day like it's your last. The heartbreak of cancer is the trauma of watching your loved one slowly disappear into death.

This is when I learned about the importance of "zero fucks." Brett's best friend Aaron was there every day and watched me apologize to every person who walked through the door. As an empath, I felt all of their pain and wanted to comfort them with apologies. After a few days, Aaron pulled me aside in the hallway, grabbed my shoulders, looked me in the eyes, and commanded, "Stace, stop fucking apologizing to everyone. You aren't killing him. It's not your fault. It's not your job to make other people feel better. You have 'zero fucks' to give any of these people. Say it! 'Zero fucks!'"

I tentatively looked at him and smiled, quietly repeating, "Zero fucks?"

"No! It's not a question, Stace. It's a fucking statement. Say it! 'I give zero fucks!'"

"I give zero fucks."

"Say it again, louder! 'I GIVE ZERO FUCKS!'"

"I GIVE ZERO FUCKS!"

"Good, now go be with your husband and stop fucking apologizing."

We both knew Brett would want the room to be filled with laughter, jokes, and lively music, things we valued our entire life together. So, in the eight days in the hospital, Aaron and I made this happen as often as possible. Aaron was one of the most loyal, true friends that Brett had. He came every day to be with him, joke with him, read to him, and so on. On day 6, he came into the hospital room, blasting Ludacris, opening up all the blinds, and letting the sunshine in. He raised Brett's bed up to a height that would allow him to give Brett a proper shave. "He's gotta look good for Jesus!" he cried, raising his arms up and stretching his wingspan like the great royal albatross. His presence filled the room to rekindle Brett's dwindling spirit.

Over the course of eight days, the life drained out of Brett. He stopped walking around the halls of the palliative care floor after day 3, and he couldn't speak after day 5. He would respond with hand squeezes up until day 6. But Brett's heart was so strong and healthy, it just wouldn't stop.

As Milky Chance sang, "I hope they didn't get your mind, your heart is too strong anyway..."

The night nurses rocked. They knew death, and they knew how to keep someone comfortable, letting the golden pain medicine flow through him to soothe his soul. The day nurses sucked. They worried about protocol and liability. They limited morphine to the very restricted and monitored amount. The day nurses suggested that maybe Brett needed to be alone to die, saying, "Some people won't go unless they are alone." Exhausted and hoping they were right, I agreed to leave him completely alone on night 6, knowing intuitively it was wrong. I was breaking my promise to hold his hand so he wouldn't be alone when he died. But our friends were in town for the holidays to visit family, and they suggested we all go out together and celebrate his life.

I will never forget that night.

First, the Bears Fuck Shit Up rallying crew tattooed B.F.S.U. on our bodies to honor him. Then we went to a swanky bar that he would have loved and ordered continuous rounds of drinks and shots for everyone. We drank our asses off, honoring Brett's natural ability to get everyone else piss drunk around him for fun. I found myself laughing, crying, and, at my lowest point, manically swallowing the half-finished glasses of the round of rosé I had ordered for everyone that no one actually wanted. With no food in my system, having drunk very little in the last two years of his fight, and surrounded by close friends, I was hammered in true collegiate-student-athlete-binge-drinking fashion.

Then I got a call from my mom. My sister was in labor. "Fuck!" I looked at my brother and said, "We gotta go. I promised Lish I would be in the room. We have to go now!"

We ordered an Uber that would drive us the seventy-five miles to the hospital in Escondido, and I proceeded to throw up in the bushes before we got in the car. One hundred and ten dollars later, we stumbled into the hospital, announcing our arrival to see our niece being born. The kind ladies on the maternity floor reception area smiled at each other, bought us vending-machine tuna salad sandwiches and water, and recommended we lie down on the couches to sleep until they opened up for visitors at 8:00 a.m. Exhausted and smelling like the French Quarter in the daytime, we thought this sounded like a magnificent idea.

The next morning, thankfully Lish was still in labor when they let us in to see her. I stood by her side, holding one of her legs while her husband, Lucius, held the other as she pushed. Karma is a bitch. I had been teasing Lucius for weeks about how he was going to pass out when he witnessed Lish in labor. This was their first baby, and I had the audacity to pretend like I knew what I was doing because I had already had a kid (high as a kite from the labor medication, of course). Having a child via C-section and lots of drugs does not compare to watching your niece's head crowning in your sister's vagina. *Holy shitballs!*

I was the one who dropped to the ground. Hungover, dehydrated, and exhausted, my knees buckled, everything went black, and I knew I had to lie down. I had felt this way before, remembering my dad's four-hour haircut episode. I lay on the floor, and the nurses immediately attended to me. My sister, in all her crowning vagina glory, shouted, "Really?! You are supposed to be my cheerleader. I'm the one having the baby here! This is ridiculous!"

Sipping a kid's boxed apple juice, with the help of the nurses, I made it to the window seat bench and lay down. "I can cheer you on from here! Keep going, you're doing great!" I laughed and cheered.

"Oh, shut up!" She jokingly laughed back.

Gracie was born early in the morning on December 21, 2016, the winter solstice and shortest day of the year. The same day, sixteen years earlier, my sister and I got our first tattoos together in Berkeley to bond in sisterhood. And December 21 now and forever will be the day before Brett died.

Gracie was glorious, healthy, and such a joy—bound by such love, surrounded by family, *and* tied to such sadness. For me, her birthday is eternally linked to the passage of time without Brett. And as time has passed, I admit her birthday hasn't gotten easier, but the triggers are familiar and expected. I have learned to embrace them and breathe through them when they take over my body.

A few hours after Gracie's birth, I got the call from Brett's brother John, who had stayed every day in the hospital to help and be with his brother. He shared with me that when he walked into the room that morning, Brett lifted his arms toward him. He hadn't moved in thirty-six hours. My heart began to beat frantically. The course of adrenaline rushed through me, awakening my soul and lasering my focus to one thing: *I should be there.* "You should get back here," John calmly stated, with the voice of a man who has witnessed and compartmentalized too many friends' deaths as a badass Navy Seal. The adrenaline coursed through me as I Ubered back to the hospital. *Please don't die before I get there,* I prayed.

The lyrics so eerily mirroring our experience kept running through my mind: "We need to fetch back the time they have stolen from us..."[36]

When I arrived late that afternoon, I asked John if I could have the night alone with Brett. We hadn't been alone together yet, due to all the visitors and family support staff holding his hand so I could sleep in the hospital room in small shifts. "Sure, Stace," he said, "whatever you need."

And that's when I knew I had to dance. I shared the whole story of the night before with him. I held his hand and told him about the tattoos, and the drunk celebratory toasts in his honor. I told him about Gracie being born and how beautiful and healthy she was. And I told him I was ready for him to go. I prayed to God, *Please take him. Please release him from this body, this pain, and give him peace.* I prayed for him to go, because I knew it was what he needed. And I danced.

I blasted "Stolen Dance" by Milky Chance and danced. I did my stupid dance that he always laughed at and made fun of me for, with my feet together, arms at my side, chin and chest out, shaking my ass, singing, and smiling.

"Stoned in paradise, shouldn't talk about it..."[37]

I danced with tears of joy and pain running down my cheeks. I would be strong for him. There was no way I was going to be a weak, selfish, "poor me" wife while he died. I refused to make him feel guilty for the shitty cards he was dealt. He was going to go to heaven, and I was celebrating the amazing way he chose to live every day, in spite of the cancer that sucked the life out of him.

I lay with him that night and held his hand. His breathing slowed down remarkably—only two to three breaths a minute. I said good night and closed my eyes. My body crashed from the chaos and emotions of the previous twenty-four hours of drunken debauchery and new life.

The last eight days of difficult goodbyes and his physical deterioration. The last ten weeks of Brett's aggressive decline. And the last two years of the fight. I exhaled and slept. He exhaled and slept.

On December 22, I woke up at 3:15 a.m. and knew he was gone. I felt so much relief and so much sadness. A quiet peace filled my heart, knowing he was no longer in pain. He had told me he was ready to go. As much as he wanted to stay for us, he knew ultimately God was calling him back. My prayers were answered, and I hated God for it.

# PART 4: AIR

*"Drumsound rises on the air, its throb, my heart. A voice inside the beat says, 'I know you're tired, but come. This is the way.'"*

—Rumi[38]

# Mermaid Mafia

When Brett died, BFSU started to fade. His death created an immeasurable amount of grief that we all processed in our own ways. He had started the group two years prior. He had led the group daily with check-in messages that would start the humorous banter. Sometimes I joined in; sometimes I didn't. Without his fighting spirit, the rallying crew started to disperse. We all became busy with our own daily lives and we all grieved in different ways. The fight was over. When couples have friends in common and later divorce, the friends inevitably choose sides. However, in this instance, Brett and I weren't divorced. He was gone, and the BFSU crew couldn't choose the dead guy. So, they were left with me, and I was terrible at keeping in touch, even before I was drowning in my own grief. The BFSU group messages slowed down and then stopped. Unfortunately, I felt like I lost the strength of those friendships over time. And I know I played a part in that further loss. Grief does fucked-up things, and there is always unexpected collateral damage from death. Unlike Brett, the phone was *not* my superpower.

## July 2012, Age 30

Brett was the mastermind behind many things, and one of those things was bringing the "Mermaids" together. He recognized a group of women in my life who were powerful and resilient. He and I had traveled with Kyla to the 2012 London Olympics to watch our friends compete. He witnessed firsthand the strong bonds among us women that we'd formed through our USA Swimming National Team adventures. We hung out at the Olympic House with a few of my Sydney teammates to watch the games and enjoy the perks of being an Olympic alum, which included free food and drinks and the opportunity to hang out with our previous Cal teammates who were competing in the games.

We connected with incredible people who participated in and, therefore, appreciate the games in a different way than the general population. As the saying goes, "Once an Olympian, always an Olympian." There was a commonality among us that made it so enjoyable to be together, no matter how much time had passed. Brett recognized how incredible these ladies were and began to enrich the soil of our friendships. He wanted Kyla to be influenced by these high-caliber women of character and positivity.

## October 2013, Age 32

Heather Petri was one of these incredible women and she came back into our lives serendipitously in 2013. After the 2012 London experience, Heather Petri and I were inducted into the UC Berkeley Athletics Hall of Fame together in 2013. Our athletic careers at Cal had overlapped by two years. She is a four-time Olympian (2000, 2004, 2008, and 2012) and a bronze, multi-silver, and gold medalist. And ultimately, she is a positive force who radiates joy and strength. Brett and I reconnected with her immediately during the Hall of Fame induction weekend in October. We found ourselves with my family and her entire college water polo team marching up Durant Avenue, cheering as we walked to the football game.

As Heather's "teammates for life" performed the California Spell-Out, two-and-a-half-year-old Kyla, who sat on Brett's shoulders, caught on and continued the cheer by yelling at the top of her lungs with her arms raised in the air, "One, two, fwee!!!" More than twenty superwomen responded with their joyful team gusto, "Go Bears!" over and over again. We were proud parents and secretly hoped she would be a Bear one day too. She was inevitably indoctrinated into the Cal college life with each nostalgic trip we took back to campus, and this weekend was no exception. She came with me onto the football field at halftime to be recognized, and as she played on the sidelines, I was in awe of her joyful naivety on the field, not understanding the immense honor of this experience.

When we returned to our home in Morocco, Brett and Heather kept in touch via social media after this wonderful weekend of Golden Bear fun. We'd moved overseas when Kyla was eight months old to give Brett international experience to further his career with APM Terminals, which owned the global shipping company Mærsk.

## Spring 2015, Age 33

When we returned to California from Malaysia in 2015, we moved to Balboa Island to be closer to Brett's mom and my family for the first six months of his fight. We needed family support for Kyla during the challenging daily schedule of doctor's appointments and treatments. I was so consumed in doing everything possible to keep Brett alive that I rarely took time for myself to hang with friends. I got rid of stress by going for a long run alone or taking a hot bath after I put Kyla to bed. My favorite thing to do was lie on the bottom of the bathtub with my legs up the wall. Head and torso fully submerged, I would calm myself by exhaling all my air out slowly and feeling myself sink to the bottom of the tub. Lying there, surrounded by water, sounds muted, I'd exhale my grief, which caused overwhelming emotions that I held on to so tightly through denial. This was the only place where I felt like I had some semblance of control. I could control my breath. I could slow down my heart rate and notice my thoughts. This warm, quiet space comforted me often.

Brett was processing my need for isolation differently. As I shut down, he was concurrently looking for ways to connect me with people who would be there when he wasn't. Heather had reached out because she was traveling down to Southern California in May 2015 for an event. She asked if she could stop by to see us and hang out. We went to breakfast on the island, and she spent a few hours with us connecting, playing with Kyla, walking on the boardwalk, and talking. Her positive energy lifted us up. She briefly told us about Swim Across America and encouraged me to be a part of the San Francisco swim. "The community is inspiring and well connected. You will love it!" she emphatically urged.

## Summer 2015

Heather also invited me to participate in the Trans Tahoe Relay in July 2015, the time and place where the Mermaid group was solidified. I was elated to swim on a six-person relay with Kristy Kowal, Rebecca Soni, Misty Hyman, Heather Petri, and Lexie Kelley. We joined numerous other six-person relay teams to traverse the width of Lake Tahoe in the annual swimming race, no wetsuits allowed. Kristy made "Mermaid Mafia" shirts that matched the famous Tahoe blue water. We took Kyla on the boat with us to experience the Mermaid party. We put on temporary tattoos, decorated the boat with mermaid fins, and laughed and danced through hours of fun and chilly swimming. Brett and his best friend Bob worked on the safety boat, setting buoys and guiding us at different points during the swim.

Brett wanted Kyla to have these women as role models, and he wanted me to have them as teammates for life. Our combined strength would get us through the hard times. He had a vision. He had commissioned Heather specifically to support Kyla and me, without telling me. I was so grateful for all these experiences, finding a shared joy in our passion for water and adventure, and I felt hopeful for more.

A few of the Mermaids and BFSU crew rallied around Kyla directly after Brett died. Her sixth birthday was fifteen days after his death, and intuitively she knew she didn't want to be around kids. She didn't want to have to answer any questions about his death. She asked if she could have a party with the Mermaids.

"Of course, sweetie," I said. "If that's what you want."

I texted the Mermaids, and a few were able to make it, including Heather, Lara, Lexie, and Mermaid Flower.

## December 2016, Age 35

Mermaid Flower was an angel sent from God. In early December of 2016, Brett was still alive but having an extremely hard day, not able to compartmentalize his pain, and requested I take Kyla out of the house so he could rest and save her from seeing him struggle. I decided to take Kyla to the Mermade Market in Dana Point, an artisanal craft fair selling gifts for the holidays. Mermaid Flower was adorned with an intricately handmade mermaid tail and sat under a canopy of seaweed and floating sea creatures. She had a crafting table full of mermaid-themed art projects. Kyla fell in love with her magical smile, long, sandy-blonde, salty-beach-waved hair, and attentive love. I watched from a few feet back as they connected, and my eyes filled with tears, overwhelmed by the spirit that flowed through her to Kyla. She had no idea how much Kyla and I needed her joy and love that day. She gave me her card and said if I ever wanted to contact her for a private party to give her a call.

When Kyla asked about having a party with the Mermaids a few weeks later, I thought, *Mermaid Flower should be there too.* I texted her, and we arranged to have the party at the Cove in Corona Del Mar for the second weekend in January, after Kyla's birthday—the first of Kyla's birthdays without her dad.

Mermaid Flower delivered a fantastical party for all the Mermaids involved by bringing a rainbow of colorful mermaid tails for us to wear. We played on the edge of the sea, where the cold, deep blue of the Pacific winter ocean water met the rich, dark, wet sand that reflected the sun's light through speckles of gold and silver. We basked in the sunshine, surrounded by rainbow pinwheels spinning in the wind and bright blankets scattered on the soft, warm sand. We crafted mermaid shell crowns with silver and gold glitter and paints in hues of turquoise, pinks, and purples. Placing them on our heads, we became mermaid royalty.

Mermaid Flower read an imaginative story about a brave mermaid to Kyla while she curled up in my arms. Kyla and I were both angry, lost, and full of grief. I hid it with a smile, but Kyla didn't. She listened to the story, head on my chest, frown on her face as she fought through this "celebration" day. Missing her dad, her overwhelming emotions spilled out onto the sand where we sat. My heart broke for her, but we still pushed through. Heather had given me a magnet that said, "We can do hard things," and I repeated this to myself throughout the party when I met Heather's eyes. I tapped into the mermaid power that surrounded us, and the love and support that we all needed to get through the day without Brett. Mermaid Flower felt the love among us and didn't realize the magnitude of her involvement until later. After the party, I explained the situation without Kyla hearing and thanked her for making a very sad and angry little girl's day so special.

Grieving the loss of your partner in solitude is hard enough. But grieving that same loss as a parent with young children adds an exponential layer of complexity that is challenging to navigate. "Challenging" is an understatement. How do you explain death and loss to a child? How do you prepare them for and protect them from the gut-wrenching pain of loss when you don't know what to expect yourself? The only thing I knew to do was educate myself. The more I read, the more I feared the inevitable. Would I survive my own grief and the grief of my child? I knew as a parent, my basic call to action was to keep my child alive. Would I be able to do this if I couldn't breathe myself? We all need air. And I was suffocating from the breath-hold of anticipation.

# Tear Soup

## November 2016, Age 35

Family and friends gave me books about grief during Brett's fight. One suggested I allow Kyla, who was five at the time, to draw while I talked to her about death. She prayed out loud at bedtime every night for God to "heal Mommy's eczema and Daddy's cancer." To her, they were one and the same: things her parents needed help with.

She did not associate cancer with pain and death. She didn't even have a clear understanding of what death meant. But Brett's health was deteriorating quickly, and Brett and I sensed the time had come for me to explain the possibility of his dying. Before bedtime, I sat with Kyla on the floor of her room on her pink carpet, while Brett rested in our bed across the hall. She was drawing a playground, with Daddy pushing her on the swing and Mommy riding down the slide, hands in the air, all as stick figures.

"Kyla, I have to tell you something that is hard to share," I said.

I watched her start to color a rainbow in the sky over the swings. Rain on one side, sun on the other. Like many five-year-olds, she was obsessed with rainbows. She even asked for "Rainbow" to be her nickname.

"Daddy is sick, and he's not getting better."

She continued to draw, not looking up at me. "Isn't he taking medicine?"

"Yes, but it's not helping him anymore. His body is starting to not work, and he might go to heaven."

"Okay, when will he come back?"

I paused, holding my breath. I didn't want to say the next words, but somehow, I carefully let them out. "He won't, honey." The words were so permanent when I said them out loud.

She stopped coloring. She looked up at me, tears filled her eyes, and she ran into our bedroom. She threw her body onto our bed and started crying, head down on the comforter.

"What's wrong, sweetie?" Brett kindly asked her, rubbing her back.

I looked at him with my sad, resolved eyes, and he knew I had shared the inevitable with her.

"Come here, sweetie," he said, lifting her up onto the bed. He held her to his chest and let her cry. He held space for her tears, silently giving her love in return. I watched, feet frozen to the bedroom floor, knowing I couldn't fix it and I couldn't protect her. It took every ounce of energy to move my feet, get up onto the bed, and join them. I lay there, head tucked into his armpit, silently crying too, knowing his ability to comfort us was diminishing. Soon it would be gone.

*Tear Soup* by Chuck DeKlyen was one thoughtful gift I received during Brett's fight. The children's book was written to help families learn about grief together. I didn't open it up until Brett was gone. I couldn't acknowledge that I was grieving before his death. The recipe included exactly what I wasn't ready to hear but needed to understand. To all those grieving the loss of a loved one, divorce, or something else, here is the recipe:

Tear Soup – a recipe for healing after loss

Helpful ingredients to consider
· A pot full of tears
· One heart willing to be broken open
· A dash of bitters
· A bunch of good friends
· Many handfuls of comfort food

- A lot of patience
- Buckets of water to replace the tears
- Plenty of exercise
- A variety of helpful reading material
- Enough self care
- Season with memories
- Optional: one good therapist and/or support group

Directions:
Choose the size pot that fits your loss.
It's okay to increase pot size if you miscalculated.
Combine ingredients.
Set the temperature for a moderate heat.
Cooking times will vary depending on the ingredients needed.
Strong flavors will mellow over time.
Stir often.
Cook no longer than you need to.
...
Serves: One[39]

## December 22, 2016, Age 35

The day Brett died, it started raining and didn't stop. I drove home from the hospital and picked up Kyla to take her to Yogurtland. I needed to tell her Brett was dead. I decided it would be easiest to tell her he had "gone to heaven." As the words left my mouth, I watched the innocence drain from her eyes. One second, they were full of childhood joy looking at her cup of frozen dessert overflowing with gummy bears. The next, with one simple statement, they turned dark and filled with watery grief. The silent tears fell, like rain from the sky. The Earth was crying with us, and together, we were cleansing our bodies of the pain. Eyes are a window to the soul. And something in the eyes changes when one experiences great loss. I was told I had sinister eyes after Brett died, and I knew why. I recognized other grieving souls through their eyes. I could feel their pain, even through smiles and joy; their eyes didn't lie.

The day after Brett died, it was still raining. I was driving with Kyla, who was sitting on her booster chair in the back seat. I surreptitiously stole glances at her from the rearview mirror as I navigated the road, worried about her state of mind. My thoughts wandered as I reflexively drove forward. *How is she handling the news? How can I make her feel better?*

And then I saw the answer.

"Kyla, look at the rainbow in the sky." I gasped in awe and pointed to the rainbow ahead in the distance. I knew it would bring her joy to see it and added, "I think Daddy sent that from heaven for you to see."

"No, Mommy," she instantly replied. Then, with clarity and confidence, she stated, "Heaven isn't in the sky. Heaven is in our hearts. That's where Daddy is."

Tears silently flowed down my face again as I slowly began to smile. *From the mouth of babes*...they are so clear in their perspective of life. I had no idea what the future of grief for her looked like, but she was teaching me about it already, at age five.

## January 14, 2017, Age 35

It rained for three weeks straight when Brett died and then miraculously stopped the day of his memorial. I woke up at 3:00 a.m. and jumped on my spin bike. I knew I needed to approach this day as a celebration of him, and I was going to need endorphins and feel-good neurotransmitters to get through it. Brett had requested that all of his friends and family get on a fishing boat out of Newport Landing to celebrate his life and spread his ashes. He wanted his body to return to the sea, where he'd felt the most at home when he was alive.

His friend from childhood, Devo, drove the *Nautilus* for us that day. He had paralleled Brett's fishing adventures and had worked his way up from pinhead to boat captain, just like Brett. He knew Brett's favorite secret fishing spots that captains often coveted in the fishing business.

The large whale-watching boat was escorted through Newport Harbor by two yellow eight-man Empacher rowing boats from the Orange Coast College crew team. Brett had rowed for them as an athlete prior to rowing for Cal and had returned to volunteer as a coach for the two years of his fight with cancer. He had made an impact on the program with his relentless tenacity to guide them to be better rowers and men. To honor him at the memorial, both boats only had seven men plus the coxswain in the boat. They had intentionally left the fifth seat—Brett's seat—empty to acknowledge his passing. The tribute ended as they stopped at the mouth of the harbor and the rowers performed a call-and-response cheer with the people on the *Nautilus*:

"One, two…"

"Go Coast!"

"One, two…"

"Go Coast!"

We felt like a team. We were all in this together, and Brett had reinforced through the sport of rowing the power to unite us in life and in death.

## May 19, 2018

Coast Crew ultimately named a boat after Brett. On the day of the christening, I gave this speech to honor him and the team he gained so much from and, in turn, served with all he had:

The first time I went to a rowing competition was a Cal vs. Stanford dual. Brett and I were friends at the time, and he asked me to come watch. As the boat passed by, I admired the power and synchronicity of the eight men in the boat. They were so technically sound that they seemed one with the boat. A machine, powerful, balanced, clearing puddles with ease. The rowers spoke of the boats with admiration and respect. I watched as they dominated the competition in a vessel built for grace and speed.

After the race, the men carried the boat out of the water and began to wash it down. Their love for the boat was clear to anyone who observed them carefully tend to its needs. Later, Brett explained to me that he rowed in the engine room, the middle seats of the boat that created the most power, impressing me with his confidence and strength. Brett's passion for rowing was one of the first things that made me fall in love with him.

He once shared with me a memory to explain his love for the sport:

When Brett was training at Cal, the team would practice at a water reservoir called Briones on special Saturdays. He explained to me that they weren't allowed to touch the water, so as to not contaminate it. However, they received special permission to row on top of it because their head coach, Steve Gladstone, was a master of words and charm and seemed to make the impossible happen often. Brett described that being out there on the water was a form of meditation. Sunshine out, no wind, surrounded by trees, water clear as glass, he would row and listen to the sound of the oars catch, push, and release the water in a mesmerizing rhythm. A rhythm that he was addicted to.

We shared a love for the water that made our bond strong. Strong bonds are common in rowing. Brett's best friends all rowed with him in his Coast crew boat: Aaron, Luke, Dan, Sam, Bob...these men toiled in the boat together. They pushed themselves, learning the hard lessons of adversity and failure. Gaining confidence, strength, and loyalty in each other with each stroke they took together as a unit. These bonds were formed in the boat and carried them through their lives together. Through graduation, relationships, marriages, babies, life, and death. I watched these men stand by Brett as their teammate and their friend during his two-year battle with cancer. Always providing an ear to listen, a joke to laugh, or a wrestling match that never ended well.

This boat shapes boys into men. It develops champions. This gorgeous boat, with his name displayed prominently on the side, is the most accurate way to honor Brett Winfield: a champion in rowing, champion in marriage, champion in fatherhood, champion in friendship, champion in family, champion in life, and champion in death. I know through my faith that his spirit will power this boat, not only to win, as we all know Brett loved to do (even if he had to cheat...in golf, not rowing of course, hahaha!) but also to develop the men that have the privilege of moving it through the water, catch, pull, release...clearing puddles...God bless this boat! Amen!

## January 14, 2017

As the *Nautilus* left the harbor, we cruised down the coastline to Crystal Cove. The rain had stopped that morning, and the sunshine brought a warmth to the day that only God can offer. As the sky turned hues of bright oranges and reds, we spotted a dolphin that joyously jumped out of the dark Pacific swells. I felt Brett's spirit smiling with us.

Grief has taught me that in moments of pain you can simultaneously feel joy. It's not one or the other. Your love for your person is ultimately linked to all emotions. The greater the love, the greater the joy, and the greater the love, the greater the pain. They are one and the same. To love is to be human, *and* to lose is to be human. Love and loss unite us all. And so, we all must make soup.

# Bears' Den

I didn't have a pot big enough to collect all the tears for my soup. So, I kept them inside. I didn't want to cook. I didn't want to do anything. I shut the lid tight on my grief, like a pressure cooker, and prayed it wouldn't explode and cause collateral damage—especially around Kyla. I was so fearful I would hurt her if I showed her my pain.

Children's flexibility and innocence give them a strength adults can't imagine. These qualities make a child so resilient in the face of adversity. The ability to relax your body and bounce when falling prevents breakage. When you hold your body tight and are rigid, you shatter on impact.

When Brett died, I felt like a million broken pieces inside, held together by my muscle tension and denial. I found every possible way to distract myself from feeling.

## December 22, 2016, Age 35

First, I hibernated. After he died, for three days leading up to Christmas, I stayed in bed at my parents' house. I slept more than anything else. Kyla joined me for some of the time when she wasn't visiting with her new cousin, Gracie.

## New Year's 2016, Age 35

Then, for New Year's Eve, I distracted myself by driving Kyla to Mammoth to hibernate in the snow. Kyla played outside with her Aunt Pharaba and threw snowballs. She was mesmerized by a giant icicle that Brett's brother, whom Kyla called "Uncle Alley," broke off the side of his A-frame to give her. I watched from inside, not wanting to move. I watched her joy, smiled at her as she shared her treasures and creations with me through the closed sliding-glass door, and felt nothing. I was numb. I didn't want to actively participate in life. I was frozen like the snowman Kyla sculpted outside.

## January–March 2017, Age 35

When we returned home from Mammoth, Kyla and I slept together in my bed for three months. I was the mom who'd made her sleep in her own bed from infancy. I was mindful that I would crush her with my consistent nighttime movement, and Brett and I wanted her to learn how to soothe herself to establish independence. But I didn't believe she should soothe herself about Brett's death. Shoulds lead to shame. She was scared to sleep alone, and I knew my presence would comfort her.

Children need their parents' presence more than anything else. Sitting quietly together and holding space for a child to grow is a gift. Shared time is our biggest resource.

So for three months, she slept next to me. Every single night for three months, I was startled awake by her long arm swinging around and smacking my face while she slept. Every single night, she unconsciously slapped me awake to see if I was still there. This fear of abandonment existed deep in her subconscious and caused her body to thrash while she slept. And it was a constant reminder for me that Brett was gone.

However, similarly to when she was an infant, after three months, I was losing my shit from sleep deprivation. I knew I couldn't participate in this nightly routine anymore or I might kill her. So I slowly weaned her from my bed and encouraged her to sleep in her own room. I scaffolded the support, knowing it would be a process to change the habit she had grown to love. First, I cuddled with her in her bed until she fell asleep. I wasn't able to fall asleep easily, which is a common symptom of grief, so even if this took hours, I was willing to sacrifice the time to help her sleep alone again. Over time, I shortened the period I spent next to her while we cuddled, and eventually it became normal for her to sleep without me again.

To this day, I still cuddle with Kyla every night. We bring each other a sense of comfort with the routine. We are bonded by shared loss. When Brett was dying, I cursed myself for pushing him to have a child. I'd joked that I would need a part of him when he died, not believing he actually would. And then he did. As time passed, I realized Kyla's existence kept me from dying too. And I have learned to show her my tears. I was doing it wrong. You shouldn't cook tear soup alone. Kyla and I had to cook the soup together. *And* I believe the serving size needs modification. Although each person might need a different size pot and various ratios of the ingredients, it should not be eaten alone. We need to eat the soup together. This soup is bottomless and will heal the world if it's shared. I am intentionally sharing it with you through this book and beyond. I can't wait to sit at your table and heal together.

# Grief-Widow Wives

## December 20, 2016, Age 35

"I've lost a lotta people in my line of work," Brett's brother John admitted. "I've had to give the news to too many grieving widows that their husband was not returning. It's not easy. But the things you're going through now will help you comfort others in the future. You'll understand what they're going through, and you'll be able to help them." John and I sat together during Brett's last eight days in the hospital and connected through conversations while Brett lay unresponsive in the bed. John was modeling his message to me through his actions, by doing in that moment what he predicted for my future. He practiced comforting others from his own grief experiences and was summoning me to do the same down the road. He might not have known it at the time, but his words were unforgettable and important to me. He gave me a sense of purpose as I slowly walked through my grief.

## January 2017, Age 35

I joined a support group called GriefShare,[40] which was an educational and support service hosted biannually at local churches all over the country. This support group was so much more than the religion practiced in the place of worship where we sat. God's messages were ever present when we gathered together, forming a valuable spiritual connection. We met once a week for thirteen weeks, sitting around a table with people who had lost the same relationship in their life, either a husband, a wife, a parent, a sibling, or someone else.

My friend had connected me with the leader of the widows' table, Susanna. She encouraged me to come, although I was reticent, and I leaned into part of the Lululemon Manifesto that I used as a daily mantra: "Do one thing a day that scares you."[41] The GriefShare program gave me the resources to learn about the process of grief and normalize it.

It also gave me a safe place to laugh, cry, and celebrate my dead husband without people cringing. Similar to Nora McInerny's creation of the Hot Young Widows Club, a support group for grief allows the space for people who "can talk about their dead person and say things that the other people in their life aren't ready or willing to hear yet."[42] Most people don't know how to respond. It's common to hear "I'm sorry" or "What can I do to help?" This question was debilitating for me. I didn't know what I needed, or even how to help myself, so this common response fucking enraged me. I thought (to myself, of course), *Why do I have to figure out what I need?! I have no fucking idea what I need... AND, why do I have to manage YOU helping me?*

More than once, I held back the urge to say, "Fuck off!" to people who asked how they could help. I was angry but knew better than to take it out on people who didn't understand. The people who helped the most didn't ask... they just did stuff. I had no idea how to ask for help, so I was extremely grateful when it arrived without request.

My connection with the women in the GriefShare support group was not forced. It immediately felt so organic and natural. They helped me recognize and anticipate ways I would need help and how to ask for it.

The first night at GriefShare, I sat around the table with the other widows. I was the youngest by thirty years—me and all the "grannies." They talked about how hard it was to live without the person with whom they had spent the last forty-plus years. It was all they had ever known. Many of them, due to their age, had only one intimate relationship in their life, and that person with whom they shared *everything* was now dead. The fear of living alone came up as a topic one week, and one of the ladies asked if anyone had an old pair of their husband's boots. "I want to set them outside on my doorstep so strangers assume the man of the house is home," she admitted. I looked at her and giggled, thinking about the various pairs of "skis"—as Brett's shoes were nicknamed due to their size— in my closet that my husband had left behind.

"I can help," I said. "My husband had size-15 shoes, and you know what they say about big shoes..." My dramatic pause had a few of the grannies snickering before the punchline and helped me identify the dirty minds, like myself. "Big socks," I said. "That was my husband's favorite joke." The elderly women all laughed together. "I would love to give you his boots. They would scare anyone away."

"Oh, thank you, sweetie."

"You're welcome."

When the ladies started talking about the possibility of dating or starting a new relationship, my ears perked up. I was thirty-five with a strong sex drive and knew I couldn't be a solitary widow forever.

"Men our age are only looking for two things," one of the ladies smiled as she shared, "a nurse or a purse. I'm not interested in being either one. I'm good with my grief-widow wife." She looked at the woman sitting next to her at the table. They had walked in together and were clearly friends. "Our husbands died one day apart, and we help each other out with things around the house. We just put in a new doorframe together." They looked at each other with pride. Their synchronous timeline of grief and friendship was surprising and admirable.

## Halloween 2017, Age 36

She was dressed in all black. Her turtleneck rose to connect with her jet-black hair, and her dark sinister eyes and high cheekbones were a deadly combination of beauty and darkness, contrasted by the brightness of her smile.

Trish was a good friend to my next-door neighbor. She was visiting him for Halloween, sitting at his kitchen counter on a high barstool, working on her laptop when I walked into his house. I was dressed up in my painted-on pleather catsuit, wearing nothing underneath. I didn't give a fuck about other people's judgment. Zero fucks. I was still numb and living hard.

When grief woke me up at 3:00 a.m., I would jump on my spin bike in the garage to quiet the gremlins in my mind. The endorphins and neurotransmitters released from exercise helped me feel better. Without an appetite and excessive, consistent movement, my hot grief body was in full effect. I couldn't stop moving: #cantstopwontstop. My physical exhaustion helped me fall asleep, and then inevitably the grief would wake me up at 3:00 a.m., and I would do it all again. Rise up, pray, burn.

Trish and I had something in common. Our husbands died three days apart. We were on the same timeline of our grief journey and became grief-widow wives the instant we met, eight months after we became widows. We both loved hot yoga and would drip the toxic thoughts and feelings out of our pores in a 105-degree room to reset our nervous systems. She understood me, and I understood her. No one wants to be in the widows' club. It is something you never wish upon anyone. But thank God we have each other.

## February 2019, Age 37

Then our widows' club gained another member. Brett's brother Christopher Allen passed away unexpectedly two years after Brett. Another family loss. Another wonderfully loving human gone too soon. His wife, Pharaba, had no choice but to join Trish and me in the club. The cost to join was gnarly, and you couldn't cancel the membership no matter how much money or negotiating power you had at your disposal. She was starting her own journey of grief, and we were able to bring her comfort and connection. We guided her and shared our acquired wayfinding skills, which we'd learned from navigating a similar path.

In grief, each person encounters obstacles on their path specific to their experience, but the general terrain is the same for all. It's full of steep and unpredictable changes in elevation. There is always a part of the path that exists on the edge of a thousand-foot cliff, with rocky waters below, and everyone feels at times that they might lose their footing and fall...or jump. Trish and I could warn Pharaba about the terrain. Our presence alone reinforced the truth that we hadn't succumbed. There are moments everyone considers jumping off to be free from the pain, but those walking with you in the club remind you to keep going. This shared connection brings comfort and was exactly what John was talking about with me in the hospital when Brett was dying. You, who are grieving, have the ability to comfort others who are grieving too. It's the only benefit of the membership.

I lay quietly with Pharaba when she crawled into her own bear's den, knowing just my presence was enough. Nothing needed to be said. Silence was the most powerful tool I could use to allow space for her to sit with her grief. Now, as Pharaba felt alone and abandoned without her partner, Trish and I reassured her that she wasn't alone. She had us. We listened as she cried and held her close, knowing her chosen person of comfort was gone. And she did and does the same for us. We reach out in anticipation of hard days—our partners' death days, birthdays, and holidays—as well as at random times with silly emojis and check-ins. We call each other when we need to laugh, cry, or share a morbid joke that other people would judge us for. We are grief-widow wives bonded through loss and shared vulnerabilities.

In a TED Talk, author Nora McInerny said that we don't move on from grief. She shared a beautifully sarcastic and vulnerable narrative about the loss of her husband Aaron:

> I haven't moved on, and I hate that phrase so much, and I understand why other people do. Because what it says is that Aaron's life and death and love are just moments that I can leave behind me—and that I probably should. And when I talk about Aaron, I slip so easily into the present tense, and I've always thought that made me weird. And then I noticed that everybody does it. And it's not because we are in denial or because we're forgetful; it's because the people we love, who we've lost, are still so present for us. So, when I say, "Oh, Aaron is ..." It's because Aaron still is. And it's not in the way that he was before, which was much better, and it's not in the way that churchy people try to tell me that he would be. It's just that he's indelible, and so he is present for me.
>
> Here, he's present for me in the work that I do, in the child that we had together, in these three other children I'm raising, who never met him, who share none of his DNA, but who are only in my life because I had Aaron and because I lost Aaron. He's present in my marriage to Matthew, because Aaron's life and love and death made me the person that Matthew wanted to marry. So I've not moved on from Aaron, I've moved forward with him.[43]

Loss is not something you get over. We continue to love our partners through death and beyond. As McInerny put it, "Grief doesn't happen in this vacuum; it happens alongside and mixed in with all of these other emotions."[44] We can only move forward. And my grief-widow wives and I walk forward, hand in hand, through all the ascents and descents that continue to happen on our path. Our grief journey will only end when we die. Time alone doesn't heal. Healing occurs through awareness, understanding, proactive human connection, therapeutic practices, and grace—grace for yourself and grace for others.

# Mac and Cheese

Grief is no joke. It is invasive, pervasive, and consistent. It doesn't get better over time. That's bullshit. If you've ever said that to anyone, you are the lucky jackass who has never experienced grief. And yes, it makes me angry when other people don't understand. But through my anger, I smile and say, "Thank you," knowing I can't blame people for what they don't know. Time doesn't fix grief. You just learn to manage it.

Every time my daughter passes a milestone—her first day of school each year, birthdays, Christmases, losing a tooth, etc.—my stomach churns, digesting the same pain of disappointment and sadness. I've learned to recognize it. I think, *Hello, friend, here we are again. Thank you for showing up. By the way, I still hate you. (Ironically, I love you too, but... shhhh, don't tell anyone.)*

In a strange sadistic way, grief keeps the connection to your loved one alive. I feel Brett when I grieve. I feel him near me, in the same room, making me laugh, saying, "Stace, are you crying again?! Seriously, suck it up!" (We had a competitive dynamic, and tears were his kryptonite, so I'm still making him pay for leaving me. *Who's laughing now, sucka?!*) Connection is empowering, and I never want to lose the connection to someone I love, even if their body is gone.

Grief is one thing. But grief and PTSD will Fuck. Your. Shit. Up!

Dr. Martin E.P. Seligman outlines the criteria for diagnosing PTSD in his book *Flourish*, from the fourth edition of the *Diagnostic and Statistical Manual of Mental Disorders (DSM)*:

—309.81 DSM-IV Criteria for Post-traumatic Stress Disorder—
A.  The person has been exposed to a traumatic event.
B.  The traumatic event is persistently reexperienced.
C.  Persistent avoidance of stimuli associated with the trauma and numbing of general responsiveness.
D.  Persistent symptoms of increased arousal.
E.  Duration of the disturbance (symptoms in Criterion B, C, and D) is more than one month.
F.  The disturbance causes clinically significant distress or impairment in social, occupational, or other important areas of functioning.

An important qualifier...is that the symptoms must not be present before the trauma.[45]

Four years after Brett died, I found myself in the same cycle of trauma. Every year, from September 30, which was his last good weekend, until December 22, I experienced triggers daily that would bring on anxiety, panic attacks, and the inability to sleep or breathe.

Dr. David Hamilton explains the mind-body connection and how our thoughts affect the chemistry of our bodies:

> Your brain responds to a stressful situation by releasing stress hormones. But your brain also releases the stress hormones when you remember a past stressful event or even when you vividly imagine one. Whether you're really there in the stressful situation, you're remembering it or imagining it, is all much the same to your brain. It releases stress hormones each time...So, you produce stress hormones because of how you feel, regardless of whether you're there (in the stressful situation) in person or there in your mind.[46]

By year 4, I'd gotten better at managing the triggers of grief. But the PTSD triggers were screaming at me, "We aren't going away! Go get help!"

I knew I needed to do something about it. Who wants to break down in the middle of the grocery store when looking at the bottle of Bai water, remembering this was the only thing he could keep down at the end of his life? Or when you find a bag of Epsom salts under the bathroom sink and are reminded of the time he took a bath, his body swollen with tumors, hoping the warm water would relieve his pain— when he couldn't even lift himself out of the bathtub, this superhuman of a man now weak from dying a slow death? These triggered memories made my throat constrict, my eyes burn, and my stomachache. I needed these memories to get out of my body. The physical pain from mental anguish sat deep inside my cells, like a rattlesnake hiding in the long grass, ready to strike at the most inopportune time and paralyze me with its poison.

My grief therapist suggested I try Trauma Releasing Exercises (TRE), also known as Self-Induced Unclassified Therapeutic Tremors (SUTT). This method uses physical exercises to evoke natural tremor responses in the body to release tension associated with trauma.[47] She was certified in SUTT and thought it would diminish my symptoms from PTSD. Goal -oriented and willing to try anything, I thought, *Why not?*

TRE was developed by Dr. David Berceli, a trauma therapist certified in field traumatology, neurotherapy, and psychoneurology.[48] My therapist sent me a few links to information about somatic-based therapy, and from what I gathered, it was based on science and seemed fairly accessible. Here's my understanding: All animals, including humans, store stress chemicals in their cells when they experience trauma that would induce the fight/flight/freeze response. Animals naturally release these chemicals in the wild through muscle tremors. Humans have stopped allowing their bodies to engage in this natural response because it's unacceptable to have a seizure when one gets overly stressed or afraid.

Can you imagine a mom violently shaking on the floor and the kids finding her?

"Hey, what's wrong with mom?!"

"Oh, she saw a spider."

I also understood that my muscles needed to be fatigued to experience the tremors. I giggled to my therapist, "I'm gonna need to work out first. Otherwise, it will take me a long time to fatigue my muscles."

I woke up at 3:30 a.m. and rode my spin bike as hard as I could for an hour in my garage. Twenty miles later, soaked with sweat, I felt prepared for our 5:00 a.m. virtual call. My therapist was based in the U.K. I'd originally started working with her when we were both living in Malaysia as expats. This early-morning call was the only time I felt I could be alone and not disrupted by my curious, concerned, observant daughter. I knew I didn't want her to find me in the middle of this process shaking on the garage floor. My trauma-releasing exercises would turn into trauma-*inducing* exercises as fast as she could say, "Mamán, I'm awake!"

The process was mentally challenging at first. It was difficult to walk the fine line of letting go enough to allow my muscles to shake without forcing the tremors. I wanted it to feel authentic and helpful, and my need to control everything had led me to years of holding on to all of my stress and tension. Thankfully, my therapist, V, knew this and was patient with me. She sweetly and calmly encouraged me.

The first round of this therapy brought waves of emotion. My legs shook and my psoas muscle violently rocked like a teeter totter. Psoas muscles run on either side of a human's spine. They start in the lower back just below your ribs, run alongside the spine through the pelvis, and end in the groin near the hips at the top of the femur. The function of the psoas muscle is to connect the upper body to the lower body, the outside to the inside, the appendicular to the axial skeleton, and the front to the back. It literally is the intersection of the entire body. As my psoas muscle tremors released the stored trauma in my tissues, tears streamed down my face and I couldn't catch my breath. V said, "Tell me what you are feeling."

"I'm so angry, and so sad. I didn't want him to die. I prayed for him to go, but I didn't want him to die." The sobbing and shaking continued.

For fifteen minutes, the tremors ebbed and flowed through me like gusts of wind over the open ocean. Currents of energy and whitecaps of emotion rose to the surface and escaped. The rivers of stress chemicals flowed out of my body through my tears. Gradually my tears dried, and my body returned to stillness.

I felt a sense of peace. Release. I also felt a heightened awareness of my psoas muscle. I had no idea how tight I held it all the time.

Two weeks later, I did my second session of SUTT with V. At first, I found myself lying on the floor, waiting, but nothing came. I wondered, *Did I get it all out? Why isn't it happening again?* Remarkably, I couldn't conjure up any feelings of stress from Brett's death. Frustrated, I verbalized to V, "I'm not sure if there is anything left to shake out."

"Why don't you place your hand on your body where you think you may need extra support?" she suggested.

Intuitively, I placed my hand on my throat. The moment my palm touched my neck, I flashed to a scene from my childhood. I was eight years old, and my dad was irrationally upset about something, yelling and screaming at my mom. He decided the best way to get out his anger was to pick up a ceramic casserole dish full of hot macaroni and cheese that had been placed on the table for dinner. He threw it against the wall, missing me by a few feet, and the dish shattered all over the floor. As I watched the gooey mac and cheese slowly slide down the wall, I stood frozen, unable to speak. I knew instinctively that any word I said would make it worse. So, I silently stood there—afraid, watching, waiting, hoping the anger would subside.

This memory made me catch my breath again as I lay on the garage floor. My throat constricted, and the hot stone in my stomach pulsed. "Tell me what you are feeling," V urged.

Tears ran down my face again, as I described the scene to her. "I'm afraid. I'm afraid he's going to hurt me. I can't speak."

"You're an adult now. What do you want to tell him? You can tell him now."

"I'm mad at you, Dad. I'm AFRAID to speak to you. I'm SCARED of you."

"Good. Know that his fear is *not* your fear. You don't have to hold on to it anymore. You can let it go." My legs began to shake as she said this—less violently than the first session, but still uncontrolled shaking to release the emotions stored inside.

When I came out of this session, I experienced an increased ability to speak up for myself. And every time I did, I thought, *It's that easy?*

Something remarkable happened a few weeks later.

I was struggling with a relationship, and I had recently confided in my mom who had then told my dad. My dad decided to call me to manically talk *at* me about it for fifteen minutes. I sat and silently listened to him as tears began to well up in my eyes. Same behavior, different day. I had to tell him how I felt, and I wanted to share my experience with SUTT with him. He had to know.

"Dad," I interrupted.

He continued to talk.

"DAD!" I repeated to stop his rant. "Dad. I need you to listen. Don't talk at all; just listen to me. You haven't asked me ONCE how I am? You're assuming I'm a certain way, and giving me advice, but you don't even know how I am. Please listen. I have to tell you something."

"Okay," he stopped himself, slamming on the brakes, and finally asked, "How are you?"

I proceeded to share my experience with SUTT. It took all my strength to tell him how I felt. To tell him about my fear. To tell him I was scared of him. He listened. And he apologized.

"Stacer, I wasn't ready to be a father. I did the best I could, but I was overwhelmed. I had no idea that moment would put so much fear in you that you still carry. I'm sorry."

Tears of gratitude streamed down my face, and my throat constriction released. "Thanks, Dad," I said. "Thank you for listening. And to answer your question: I'm doing okay."

My dad's emotional growth and sincere reflection on his own trauma-inducing behavior helped my own psychological and emotional growth with regard to my relationship with him and with trauma. There is an enlightening and liberating phenomenon of post-traumatic growth (PTG) that one can embrace to improve the human condition after grief and trauma. Dr. Seligman defines this phenomenon:

> A substantial number of people also show intense depression and anxiety after extreme adversity, often to the level of PTSD, but then they grow. In the long run, they arrive at a higher level of psychological functioning than before...A few years ago, Chris Peterson, Nansook Park and I added a link to my Authentic Happiness website www.authetichappiness.org. The new questionnaire

listed the fifteen worst things that can happen in a person's life: torture, grave illness, death of a child, rape, imprisonment, and so on. In one month, 1,700 people reported at least one of these awful events, and they took our well-being tests as well. To our surprise, individuals who'd experienced one awful event had more intense strengths (and therefore higher well-being) than individuals who had none. Individuals who'd been through two awful events were stronger than individuals who had one, and individuals who had three—raped, tortured, or held captive for example—were stronger than those who had two.[49]

He goes on to describe the work that he helped to facilitate with the United States military to "create a more psychologically fit"[50] military through Comprehensive Soldier Fitness, under the leadership of Brigadier General Rhonda Cornum:

> [Rhonda] recruited two professors of psychology, to oversee the PTG module, Richard Tedeschi, the academic leader of the PTG field, from the University of North Carolina at Charlotte, and Harvard's Richard McNally. The module begins with the ancient wisdom that personal transformation is characterized by renewed appreciation for being alive, enhanced personal strength, acting on new possibilities, improved relationships and spiritual deepening, all

of which often follow tragedy...we should make the most of the fact that trauma often sets the stage for growth.[51]

To understand the best conditions for PTG in greater detail, I recommend you read the book *Flourish* by Dr. Seligman. He and his colleagues' work in the field of positive psychology to discover our potential to grow from trauma is inspiring.

Dr. Richard Tedeschi uses the Posttraumatic Growth Inventory to measure the phenomenon of post-traumatic growth. Some of the samples of growth that Dr. Seligman shares from this inventory that I resonate the most with are:

> I have a greater appreciation for the value of my own life.
> I have a better understanding of spiritual matters.
> I established a new path for my life.
> I have a greater sense of closeness with others.
> I put more effort into my relationships.
> I discovered that I'm stronger than I thought I was.[52]

I resonate with the final one most, and in full transparency, I struggle when people tell me, "God doesn't give us what we can't handle." My honest prayer sometimes is: "God, I'm strong enough. Please don't give me any more." With a better understanding of the ability to grow from trauma, I walk forward with an open heart and optimistic mind for all the experiences to come.

# The Power of Connection

The heaviness of grief weighs us down and makes it seem like we may never feel light enough to fly again. But we can choose to find inspiration all around us and feel joy, if we tap into the energy and power of connection with our community and the spiritual world that keeps us connected to our loved ones.

I felt the greatest sense of belonging in my partnership with my husband. As Owen Eastwood explains,

> To feel a sense of belonging is to feel accepted, to feel seen and to feel included...trusting we will be protected by them...These are the people we can most trust. These are the people who will have our backs in hard times. These are the people our wellbeing is tied to...When social relationships feel under threat we respond both emotionally and physically as though our survival is threatened.[53]

So of course, when our loved one's body dies and we are thrown into the insecurities of losing the connection to this source of well-being, we experience the fight/flight/freeze response. Our basic needs of survival feel unfulfilled. If we can tap into the idea that the connection to our loved one isn't lost—it has just changed form—then we can feel a sense of comfort from the "hormone soup" of belonging. As Eastwood explains: "[W]hen we experience a sense of belonging our body produces a hormone soup that enables oxytocin, serotonin, dopamine and endorphins to work their collective magic. Stress hormones are still there but in balance; our anxiety and fear are lowered and we feel calmer and safer."[54] I believe that the spirits of our loved ones continue to influence others beyond the grave. And as Kyla so poignantly shared with me, one's spirit is ever-present, even in death, in the hearts of those who love them.

Love and grief are intertwined, permanently linked to each other for all eternity. Their presence in our own being will continue long after we think we have found our happy ending and "beaten grief." In fact, some people get stuck in the symptoms of grief because it's how they continue to feel connected to those they have lost. People will unconsciously or intentionally choose to stay in the cycle of grief, but this loop of sadness can cause more pain. When you stop grieving, does that mean you've stopped loving? No one beats grief, because that would mean it no longer exists within you. This would also eliminate the love of that person within you. The ultimate goal is to find peace while living with grief in a way that causes less pain and more joy.

THE POWER OF CONNECTION

The spirit of the living goes on to something greater, which I wish I could explain through facts and science. I cannot. The knowledge of the spirit world is a deep-seated intuition that grows stronger for me through experience. As science has proven, the placebo effect is real and can heal. My belief is that Brett's spirit, and those of others I love, visit me through hummingbirds. Continuing to feel and connect to his spirit helps me find peace with grief. Every time I see a hummingbird land near me, I feel like Brett's spirit is watching me, and the hormone soup of belonging heals me. I feel Brett's spirit with me often (in my heart, according to Kyla), though I find it easier to place in something tangible like a hummingbird that I can see.

The hummingbirds started arriving in my environment and entering my consciousness after his death and continue still. They come so frequently that I no longer search for them. They find me, and I smile every time. Many cultures believe something similar. It doesn't have to be a hummingbird. People in grief have shared with me many different spirit-animal connections: butterflies, bunnies, seagulls, crickets, and more. To each his own; I won't "yuck your yum"!

## December 22, 2017

On the first anniversary of Brett's death, I couldn't sleep, so I got out of bed before the sun and went on a sunrise run past Monarch Golf Course to Monarch Beach, Salt Creek, and Strands. I was so overwhelmed about the anniversary of Brett's death that tears streamed down my cheeks as I ran. When I reached the Headlands of Dana Point, I decided to find a spot to sit and cry by myself until I ran out of tears, for fear of anyone judging me on the running path. I climbed up the rocks at the end of Strands Beach and sat against the point to watch the waves crash below as the tears flowed into the ocean.

Once the tears stopped, which felt like it took forever, I decided to run home. On the way back, a hummingbird kept buzzing back and forth in front of me, and I could hear it because my phone had died and I wasn't able to run to music as I usually did. I stopped when it did a flyby, so close to my head I felt the vibration of its wings near my ear. It rested on a tree branch and began to chirp at me. I didn't want him to leave, feeling like Brett's spirit was trying to console me, so I waited until he was done talking and flew off.

When he flew away, I continued running and realized the metaphor for my life. The run home was uphill and much harder than the run to the point. As I ran and continued to push my body, my mind knew the grief journey was not going to get easier, but I had to persevere through it. Almost to the top of the run, the hummingbird landed one more time in front of me and watched me. I was feeling better, and so I told him, "Brett, I love you, and I will see you tomorrow." I felt in that moment the freedom and faith that he was still with me, still guiding me and pushing me up the hill when things got hard.

## March 15, 2018

My favorite hummingbird story involves Kyla. She was struggling in school, and I decided to pick her up early at lunch to cheer her up with a mommy-daughter date to Fashion Island in Newport Beach. My friend Ashley, who was a huge part of the BFSU crew, worked at Lululemon, and I wanted to take Kyla there to buy her something fun and see Ashley.

Before we went into the store, Kyla made a wish in the fountain, which was something she had frequently done with Brett when he was alive. We spent a long time in the store talking with Ashley and trying on clothes. I felt Brett's presence there with us. When he was alive, he would take me to Lululemon and buy me yoga pants as a gift, and I knew he would be so happy watching Kyla try on these clothes like he used to do with me. I thought to myself, *He would have loved to do this with Kyla too,* and that thought caused a deep visceral ache in my gut that I did my best to ignore.

When we left the store, Kyla seemed sad. When I asked her why, she said, "My only wish was that Daddy would come as a hummingbird to see me in the store." Feeling the guilt of previously sharing this spiritual representation of Brett with her and knowing it was bringing her pain, I tried to reassure her and suggested that maybe he was there and we couldn't see him.

Later that night, Ashley called me to check in and shared a story with me. Apparently, right after we left, the customers noticed a hummingbird stuck in the store. "You missed the excitement," she said. "Right after you left the store, there was this hummingbird buzzing up high around the ceiling. We spent thirty minutes trying to get it out of the store. It was wild."

Ashley didn't know about Kyla's wish, or that I thought Brett's spirit was a hummingbird. She had just called to share the silliness of the day. But I couldn't believe it: he had been there the whole time.

Connection to our loved ones who have passed on is important. And connection to the ones still alive is equally important. Sharing grief with the community is powerful, and sharing hummingbird stories created stronger connections for me. When I shared my belief with someone that Brett's spirit was a hummingbird, they would smile and make the connection as well. Then they would reinforce the connection by pointing out hummingbirds to make me smile or giving me a hummingbird ornament as a gift. It kept our connection to Brett alive, in these symbolic spirits that existed among us daily. Whatever spirit animal your loved one embodies, make sure to share it with others, to keep the connection alive and strong even when time passes and most people forget the day they died or their birthday. You never forget those days, and that's fantastic and painful all at the same time.

We can further relate to Eastwood's idea of a sense of belonging when we connect to the human condition of grief and confirm shared beliefs and ways to behave with others who grieve. My grief-widow wives, who are in my innermost circle of trust and connection, give me the deepest sense of belonging. They ultimately reinvigorated the sense of belonging that felt lost when Brett died, because we have a shared purpose, language, and understanding of each other, and we feel the need to serve each other and others who grieve.

This need to serve is a part of the hormone soup to heal because there is a chemical reward system for service. Psychologist Michael Gervais explains how our biology drives motivation to serve others:

> As Maslow explains, survival is a base need. Once that is secured, we want to help others. Our body rewards us for selfless action through serotonin, oxytocin, dopamine and endorphins—we don't get those same hits when we are only serving self-interest.[55]

Service becomes a healthy addiction: Who doesn't want to feel all those good chemicals in their body? It is healing for us and those around us. When we serve others who are in pain and can show them the beauty of their scars, we reframe their perspective. Eastwood uses the most beautiful imagery to describe this process. When his ancestors constructed the vessels to explore the seas for the greater good of the tribe,

> [t]he sacredness of the mission was evident in how they treated the trees chosen for the purpose. These trees were deemed living ancestors; they had shared the land and breath with generations of their kin... Our ancestors saw the inevitable adversity ahead and took comfort that the heart of these great trees was not at their center, but rather to the side that had faced the harshest force of nature. They understood that the most beautiful patterns in these trees resided in the places that had suffered the most.[56]

Our suffering makes us beautifully empathetic to others. It deepens our connection and strengthens us to serve. It allows us to make the greatest impact on others while the sun shines on us, and when the sun sets, we will rest with the knowledge that we are attached "to something permanent in our impermanent world"[57] because the ideas of *whakapapa* "explicitly connect us to something greater than ourselves."[58] We connect to the community around us and the spirit world of the loved ones we have lost, so we live with intention. This mindful approach to life will heal our bodies through the power of connection.

## April 2017, Age 35

A few months after Brett, died, my friend Aaron Peirsol took me paddling from the Wedge in Newport Beach, California, to Crystal Cove State Park. He saw my grief. He knew I needed to get out on the water more than I did. The overcast skies made the water a rich, dark green that winter day when we started out. As we entered the water, I felt a sense of awe. The ocean always took away my ego and connected me to something greater. The power of connection to the water through friendships brings me the greatest joy.

The heat of the sun's rays burned off the morning marine layer as we made our way down the coastline. Slowly the clear blue sky appeared engulfed in sunshine. Aaron had a destination in mind. He knew the complexities of the ocean better than anyone. He watched the wind and witnessed the current as he carefully guided us to a stopping point a few miles down. I was in for the journey. I was living each day one breath at a time. Some days, one breath at a time was all I could manage to process. Other days, the breaths came easier. Out on the water with Aaron, joy filled my being as I pushed my body through the mental anguish of death, following his lead, trusting his instinct.

We stopped at not just a rock, but an *ocean island* rock—majestic and huge, and waiting to be mounted.

"There's a place to jump off that rock if you want to," he carefully suggested.

"Really?!" My wide eyes and broad smile revealed my excitement. I contemplated the possibility of finally feeling something. I'd been pushing hard through the grief for the last few months, hoping different experiences would bring back my emotions. Not much did. I was numb and charging through life, knowing tomorrow might not come. *This might help me feel,* I thought.

"Yes. It's a little precarious to get up, but once you're on top, there's a small platform you can stand on. The guards jump off it for training." He was referring to the ocean lifeguards of Southern California who train to save people's lives every day.

I pondered, hesitating. He waited, smiling at me. His slow, kind smile was like sweet dripping honey made from wildflowers, and it had a powerful grip on my willingness to do anything he asked.

"If you want, I'll go up first, and you can watch how I do it," he said.

"Okay," I nodded.

I held on to his paddleboard as he swam toward the rock. He timed the surge perfectly, and the water lifted him up, placing his hands and feet on the rock with a gentle ease. I watched as he navigated the climb, muscles firing and releasing in a rhythmic motion that he'd internalized over years of pushing himself physically. His body and the rock became one as he reached the top of the precipice. He stood on the edge, hands on his hips. He waited for the surge—and then jumped.

"Yee-www!" he shouted.

I threw my hands in the air and laughed as he resurfaced.

"That was awesome!" I shouted to him as he sculled back toward me, head up, with a huge smile on his face.

"Your turn," he coaxed.

"Fuck yeah."

I handed him my paddleboard and entered the dark, frigid, winter water of the Pacific. I breaststroke-kicked my way to the rock, waited for the surge, and grabbed the rough barnacles mixed with sandstone and seaweed. The sharp edges of the shells painfully pushed into the bottom of my feet. The physical pain replaced my internal pain. It was cathartic. Dopamine surged through my veins in anticipation of the leap off the rock.

As I stood on the platform, looking down at the dark water, I couldn't help but remember my ten-meter jump in Iowa twenty years earlier. This was higher, but the muscle memory was there: pounding heart, gazing down at my fear again, toes curling over the edge, waiting for the moment to let go and feel. I looked out to sea and saw Aaron sitting on his long, white, prone paddleboard. Legs draped casually over the sides and hands resting on the board in front of him, he smiled up at me. He knew I would jump. He knew what I had been through. His friendship and love gave me a moment of joy in a sea of sadness. And for an instant, falling through the air, time slowed down and the grief hurt a little less.

# PART 5: DANSE VOLANTE (FLYING DANCE)

*"Le danse volante te libérera."*

—Staciana Winfield[59]

# Big Win Energy

This part of the book was the most challenging to write because I am wary of sharing what could be perceived as "solutions" to grief and trauma. I want to be clear that these are not the answers or prescriptions, but merely descriptions from my own personal experience. I am not a licensed medical professional, and I fully understand that each person should be properly diagnosed by a licensed practitioner through standardized processes for any mental health struggle. Please refrain from self-diagnosis, or even worse, diagnosing a friend, family member, or acquaintance based on this book. Each individual's needs are unique and complex, and it requires a professional healthcare provider to begin the process of diagnostic tests, care delivery, and consistent follow-ups when starting a protocol for healing.

With that said, I am leaning into the discomfort and fear of vulnerability because I do believe in the sharing of ideas and experiences to possibly help others. So please enjoy this section, read it at your leisure, and take from it what serves you. And if you need help, please seek a medical professional's consultation. There are resources in the back of this book as a starting place, including health hotlines for medical emergencies.

There is a time and a place for stillness. And there is a time and a place to move. Movement and stillness have healing powers; they are connected to energetic shifts in our nervous system. The importance is to find a balance between movement and rest, dancing along the line of well-being that connects the two, driven by self-awareness, reflection, and feedback. Our external experiences affect our internal experience and vice versa. Furthermore, what we choose to put into our bodies has significant outputs. Healthy inputs usually lead to healthy outputs. I practice this dance of balance daily, and each day the steps between the two vary. I have learned from master teachers to embrace without judgment where I am on the spectrum of rest and movement and to love the act of dancing itself. However, if stillness is not a choice—if you feel stuck in trauma, depression, or grief, or if you cannot move due to injury or mental and physical fatigue—then it is important to take baby steps to start moving when you are rested, ready, and able. In this part of the book, I'll share some ways to start moving again and ways to ask for help if you feel frozen.

I have found essential practices that make up my dance and help with the process of healing and well-being: **breathwork and yoga, movement, meditation,** *and a buffet of free and paid* **therapeutic practices**. At one point or another, all of these categories have given me a sense of control over my body and mind, and I feel better when I practice them. They help me when I'm struggling with physical sickness, grief, trauma, a hard workout, or just the minutiae of daily life. I have labeled these sections for you to easily search and learn more about my use of these practices.

In the field of positive psychology, a growing body of "research and evidence-based practices support[s] the notion of a bidirectional relationship between the mind and the body."[60] The body affects the mind, and the mind affects the body. They are not separate. With the help of mind-body therapy (MBT), which includes some of the essential practices listed, the field of positive psychology has confirmed that many people have similar positive outcomes when participating in these activities.[61] That said, to each his own. You have to find what works for you. We are all unique and masters of our own bodies. I am only an expert on myself, so please take what serves you. Listen to your body, and communicate with your doctors to help diagnose any issues. All essential practices are useful and powerful when combined and consistently utilized in ratios specific to each individual's needs.

# Yoga and Breathwork

## Fall 1999, Age 18

I hated yoga the first two weeks I tried it my freshman year at Cal. The swimmers were required to attend a yoga class for dryland training twice a week for thirty minutes, and it was painful. I couldn't touch my toes, and my body and mind were rigid. I had not made flexibility a priority in all my physical training, and my big muscles screamed at me because of the tension they held.

Yoga combines movement, meditation, *and* breathwork, so it's a three-for-one (or "buy one, get two free" if you're a discount shopper like me). The greatest yoga teachers will guide you to use your breath to help release tension in mind and body. In yoga, the more you "try" to force a pose through muscle contraction, the less progress you make. It's when you let go of the need to control the pose and you relax into it that you feel the tension melt away and your body becomes more flexible while gaining strength.

For two weeks, I struggled and was uncomfortable in all the poses, except one: Savasana. As much as I hated yoga for increasing my awareness of the tightness in my body and for making me feel inadequate, I fell in love with the last five minutes of class. It became an addiction. Savasana, or dead man's pose, is when you lie on the floor at the end of a yoga class and practice stillness. It's a form of meditation to allow your body to recover with efficiency using breathwork to slow down your body systems and increase whole-body circulation without having to fight gravity.

This is the secret to youth: increased circulation allows for healing. Children heal more quickly than adults because they move more, their heart rates are inherently faster, and more blood pumps through their bodies. More blood flow equals more nutrients to the cells of the body to reproduce and function properly. The lymphatic system, which is tied to our immunity, requires movement of skeletal muscle to fight bacteria and viruses. It cleanses our bodies the more we move.

As an athlete, I really enjoy being guided in meditation, especially as a beginner. It's like having a coach to help you when you feel underqualified or unmotivated—and it is so important to find the right coach. In guided meditation, you must find the voice that works for you. Everyone perceives sound uniquely. Some voices are grating, and some are smooth like honey. The growing body of guided meditation apps and free content on the internet allows you to find what works for you. Once you find it, practice daily. I use meditation throughout the day for short periods of time to reset. There are resources at the back of this book for a place to begin. Please connect with me to share your discovered favorites; the more we collaborate on resources, the healthier and kinder we can be in this world together.

The human body has the miraculous power to heal and wants to reach a balance, always striving for homeostasis. Our breath drives proper body function. Research supports the benefits of regulated breath, including this review from PositivePsychology.com:

> Intentional breath regulation to increase pulmonary capacity while reducing the rate of breathing cycles has been acknowledged as an effective method to improve both physical and mental health. By consciously engaging the diaphragm, the practice of slow-paced deep breathing activates the parasympathetic nervous system and inhibits the sympathetic nervous system, invoking a relaxation response and decreasing stress (Saoji, Raghavendra, & Manjunath, 2019). Studies show that deep-breathing exercises can lower depressive and anxiety symptoms (Jerath, Crawford, Barnes, & Harden, 2015) and foster emotional wellbeing (Zaccaro et al., 2018).[62]

I've personally benefited from breathwork while living with the challenges of asthma, and I continued the practice as a swimmer through hypoxic training. This training technique involves holding your breath for an extended distance and/or time and prepares the body for low-oxygen environments like the underwater portion of racing. Breath training through swimming strengthened my lungs, and my yoga practice multiplied the benefits. When grief and PTSD threw me into full-blown panic attacks the first five years after I watched my husband's body slowly die, I found breathwork to be the most useful tool to rescue me from these episodes.

When uncontrollable panic took over my body, I became paralyzed in the moment of trauma. My heart rate increased spontaneously, which created a shortness of breath, and I felt like I was suffocating even though I was standing still. With my feet stuck to the ground, the visceral pain in my gut and throat restriction made me feel like I had no control over my body. My body experienced an elevated cortisol response from my thoughts, which put me in the fight/flight/freeze mode, and this direct link between my nervous system and my physiological systems caused havoc. The connection was undeniable. Intuitively, I focused on my breath to regain control, which I had learned from years of practicing pranayama breathing in yoga.

According to Healthline, pranayama, or intentional breathing, "is the ancient practice of controlling your breath. You control the timing, duration, and frequency of every breath and [breath] hold. The goal of pranayama is to connect your body and mind. It also supplies your body with oxygen while removing toxins. This is meant to provide healing physiological benefits."[63] The body, or soma, and the mind are deeply connected and can be controlled with the breath. Practicing yoga with pranayama is equivalent to drinking from the cup of vitality.

In a moment of intense panic or anxiety, I intentionally breathe by taking easy, full inhales and extended, deep exhales to clear the thought and release the pain in my body. This practice slows down my heart rate and helps me gain control of my breath and body again. My increasing fascination with the power of breath has led me to learn and practice various breathing techniques that help me feel good, including ujjayi breathing, the Wim Hof Method, nasal-only breathing, box breathing, extended exhale diaphragmatic (belly) breathing, and more.

Dr. Peter Attia, a prominent longevity expert, talks about the importance of our *healthspan*, "how *well* you live—the quality of your years"[64] in conjunction with our *lifespan*, which he defines as, "how long you live, your chronological lifespan."[65] He goes on to say that "healthspan is typically defined as the period of life when we are free from disability or disease"[66] and adds that the second part of longevity should be our plan to "maintain and *improve* our physical and mental function."[67] The more you intentionally take deep, slow breaths full of life-giving oxygen, and the more you move, the slower you will experience a decline in your healthspan, due to increased rigidness from not moving. These exercises of breathwork and yoga help me *feel* younger as I age. At the back of this book, you'll find an extended list of resources on breathwork techniques and research if you care to take a deep dive into the data and discover the "why" of what works for you on any given day.

# Movement

*"Exercise has the greatest power to determine how you will live the rest of your life."*

—Dr. Peter Attia, *Outlive*[68]

I love to move. I am passionate about it. I have a running list of various options that I choose from to move daily depending on how I'm feeling. Some days it's running; some days it's spinning or hot yoga. The list goes on: dancing, swimming, walking, hiking, cycling, roller skating, ice skating. (If you have suggestions for movement I didn't list, let me know! I would love to try it.) My body is in heaven if I am in motion.

I know not everyone shares my opinion of movement and my experience of how it makes me feel. As my middle school students have put it while doing a sit-up routine during PE, "You know we aren't training for the Olympics, right?!"

I kindly and sarcastically reply with a huge loving grin on my face, "Oh, don't worry—I know." Most middle schoolers enjoy snarky loving teachers. It makes them feel more comfortable if you don't take yourself or them too seriously. Humor helps lighten the load of middle school social burdens.

If you're reading this and recognize you haven't moved in awhile, the idea of daily movement might seem intimidating. According to Dr. Peter Attia, "[I]f exercise is not a part of your life at the moment, you're not alone—77 percent of the US population is like you...Now is the time to change that... Going from zero weekly exercise to just ninety minutes per week can reduce your risk of dying from all causes by 14 percent."[69] Of course, starting to move after not moving is challenging. No judgment, we have all been there—even I have found myself on a movement hiatus from time to time. If you aren't able to move, breathwork is the perfect place to start.

If you are able to move a small amount without causing injury, remember slow progression of movement is key. When you begin to move again, it's normal for *everything* to hurt at first. Start small. If you can, start with five minutes of movement a day, and then increase the frequency of movement throughout the day (for example, six rounds of five minutes) or lengthen the duration of movement (add five minutes to each session to progress over time). I have a friend who changed his body mass index (BMI) drastically over the course of six months by incorporating small movements daily. He chose to do a few push-ups or squat jumps throughout the day at random intervals, while coaching on the deck or having a conversation with a friend. This is a fascinating and fun way to confuse people around you—and get stronger in small increments. You aren't limited to these examples. Any small movement will do.

Dr. Attia justifies the necessity for movement as follows:

> [E]xercise strengthens the heart and circulatory system...[it] helps the human "machine" perform far better for longer. At a deeper biochemical level, exercise really does act like a drug...it prompts the body to produce its own endogenous drug-like chemicals. When we exercise our muscles generate molecules known as cytokines that send signals to other parts of our bodies, helping to strengthen our immune system and stimulate growth of new muscle and stronger bones. Endurance exercise such as running or cycling generate another potent molecule called brain-derived neurotrophic factor, BDNF, that improves health and function of the hippocampus, a part of the brain that plays an essential role in memory.[70]

My wish for you is that you find a practice in movement that fits with where you are at this moment—and that you give yourself grace. It's okay to sit and not go outside if that's where you are that day. The early stages of grief tend to paralyze people. Just don't let yourself stay inside forever.

My hibernation period of grief lasted only a few days because I knew I needed to move. That hadn't changed for me. What *had* changed were my life circumstances. Ultimately, becoming a single mom with a young child when my husband died made it impossible to go to the gym. So instead, I set up a spin bike in my garage, and when my daughter was asleep, I rode it as hard as I could for months until it died. Then my neighbors, who recognized I wouldn't survive without spinning even for a day, set up a neighbor's bicycle on a stationary trainer in my garage until they could revive my spin bike with new parts. It was an amazing gift.

There is power in all movements. I encourage you to try something new if you can. There is beauty and joy in being a beginner and ultimately terrible at something when you start. Embrace it. Laugh at yourself. It's okay—we don't have to have it all figured out. You will connect with the people around you through your vulnerabilities. Workout classes are the best place for this if you have the ability and freedom to attend one. There is power in the community through shared experience. You can search for your local YMCA, gym, or community center for group classes. And there are many virtual online options as well for movement communities if you so desire.

# Meditation

## January 24, 2020, Age 39

"I am..."

"I am..."

"I am..."

I sat in the dark theater while listening to Mallika Chopra repeat these words to two hundred adults as she guided the professional community of St. Margaret's Episcopal School through a one-minute body scan, then repeated this simple prompt and asked us to listen to and reflect on our inner voice without judgment. My internal voice answered differently each time:

"I am...*tired*."

"I am...*scared*."

"I am...*broken.*"

"I am...*lost.*"

Tears streamed down my face as I silently sat still and felt the pain well up within me. It had been three years since Brett died, and this personal check-in was overwhelming, especially among my peers. As I worked through the feelings, Chopra continued asking more questions, and my internal voice answered.

"What do I want?" she calmly asked.

*Peace and connection.*

"How can I serve myself?" Her voice floated out to each of us with love and concern.

*Self-care, exercise, rest, prayer,* my internal voice whispered back.

"How can I serve others?" She called us to action.

*Shine my light, write my book, share my authentic voice.*

"What am I grateful for?" she asked us, understanding the power of gratitude.

The answers came to me in fragments of ideas: *Love. This day. Similar messages coming together to guide me.*

She had given me the gift of understanding intention and the importance of meditation to discover intent, which she defined that morning: "Intentions are seeds that we plant in our soul in this deep space inside of us. We don't know how it's going to manifest."[71]

I had the specific intention when I was a teenager to make an Olympic team and be the best in the world. I felt the energetic shift toward that intention with each decision and experience leading up to it. The intention had its own gravitational pull. In reflecting on writing this book, I have experienced a similar energetic shift from the power of intention and am grateful for the gift of meditation to help me identify my intentions in a way that brings self-awareness, clarity, and growth.

It is also important to note the possibility of meditation to bring up things that we don't want to feel. Chopra reflects, "I'm slightly appalled by the darkness of my internal landscape, and I'm struck by the desire to close the curtain and forget I ever glimpsed what lay behind it."[72] She advises instead of trying to escape it, we should try the process of labeling or naming. According to Dr. Dan Siegel, a clinical professor of psychiatry at UCLA, "[T]here's a biological explanation for how [naming] works. Research by his colleagues at UCLA shows that when you name an emotion or experience, it calms down the neural firing in the emotion-processing part of the brain known as the limbic system...When it comes to negative emotions, Siegel says, 'You need to name it to tame it.'"[73]

As a young athlete, I spent so much time developing my physical body and less time developing awareness of my thoughts and emotions. Most athletes' predominant focus is on the physical, and they develop a hyperawareness of their physical body—how to move it, how it feels. Athletes become aware when something is wrong with it, including injury and sickness. Practicing stillness, meditation, and body scans can help athletes develop a greater awareness and understanding of their internal landscape of thoughts and emotions and recognize when it needs attending to through self-care and therapeutic practices. Humans' somatosensory system plays a huge role in our awareness of our bodies. This large network of nerve endings and sensory receptors in the body allows us to feel touch, temperature, movement, and pain. Anyone can increase their body awareness through increased movement and guided meditative body scans. These whole-body scans are a simple way to become conscious of how your body is feeling physically, from your head down to your toes. This increased awareness develops a conscious connection with the somatosensory system. Mallika Chopra describes how to do this, in her book *Living with Intent*, with a process she calls "Intent Practice: Trusting Your Body's Messages."[74] Please check out her book for a deeper understanding of this practice, or find a guided body scan meditation online that you enjoy. The back of this book has more resources for you to discover meditative practices if it serves you.

Also, it is important to note, as recognized by the Cleveland Clinic, that people with "severe anxiety or a history of significant trauma [should] proceed carefully." The clinic quotes a doctor as advising, "As you become more aware of what's in your body, use your judgment about whether things are unmanageable...Sometimes, becoming more aware of what's happening in your body can bring up intense feelings that you may want to work through with a therapist."[75]

As a daily check-in for my body, I have a screen saver on my phone that randomly comes up in the alternating photos. It has a beautiful, calming background of shallow, clear, tropical water in which you can see the golden sand below. The words are a reminder to:

> Pause,
> unclench your jaw,
> soften your forehead,
> drop your shoulders,
> and take a deep breath.

Now, when you read this, did you try it? Did you recognize that your jaw was clenched? Were your shoulders up by your ears? Mine always are, so this visual reminder when

I'm not conscious of how I'm holding tension in my body offers a wonderful way to release it.

Within the body's somatosensory system, proprioceptors are special cells that sense the position of the different parts of the body in relation to each other and the surrounding environment, and they are found in our tendons, muscles, and joint capsules, allowing us to detect changes in muscle length and tension. Research has confirmed "that extracurricular sports activities can modify the proprioceptive map and improve proprioceptive acuity and stability,"[76] meaning the more you move, the more awareness you have of your body.

This sensory hyperawareness is useful for some purposes, like knowing where you are in space, increasing your movement literacy, or noticing when you're getting sick or developing an injury due to overuse or trauma. However, sensory hyperawareness can be overwhelming at times, like when you are in a very crowded space or feel overstimulated by sensory input. For example, at certain times of the month that correlate with my ovulation and hormone cycles, I become hyperaware of sound and light, to the point where it seems too loud or too bright and my nerves fire, causing me to overreact due to increased nervous tension.

How do we decrease stimulus to help calm our nervous systems when we are overstimulated from trauma or grief?

I have experienced a decrease in sensory input through guided meditation in a dark, warm room during hot yoga, which has increased my sense of calm and put me into a relaxed state.

In meditation, one experiences the phenomenon and healing benefits of stillness. If we lie still for long enough, we can lose the proprioception of our body. We start to lose awareness of our extremities and feel a sense of oneness and connection with the ground. Many people picture mediation as limited to yogis sitting in full lotus pose, eyes half closed for hours, in a state of enlightenment. I have to admit, if I sit this way for more than a minute, I want to crawl out of my skin and scream at the top of my lungs. There is nothing restful for me about this position, and I definitely do not reach "enlightenment" like this. However, I have found extremely restful moments during the meditative practice of Savasana in yoga.

How you choose to practice breathwork, move, and meditate will be unique to you. I have tried and discovered all different types of movement, guided meditations, and breathwork techniques. Some work for me one day and not another. The important thing is not how you do these things on any given day, but that you do them and develop a consistent practice. The more consistently you practice, the easier the techniques become, because your body adapts to the new skills. You'll recognize how beneficial your new habits are, because you'll start to feel terrible when you *don't* practice.

Full transparency: there are still moments when I don't want to move at all, even years after my grief started. Instead, I want to curl into a ball and hide from the world. That's absolutely normal—for everyone. And that feeling will pass. When I had to get out of bed for morning practice at 5:00 a.m. at UC Berkeley and it was 30 degrees outside and freezing, I would play the counting game. I would start counting from one and have to be out of bed by the time I got to five. It worked every time to motivate me. Try it!

# Therapeutic Practices

Words carry meaning, and each individual attaches different meanings to each word. The word "therapy" carries loaded meanings for each culture. Some people experience an adverse reaction to the word or idea of therapy. It is important to define it for the purpose of this book, based on its etymology and cognates. It comes from the Greek *therapeia*, meaning "curing, healing, service done to the sick, a waiting on," and from *therapeuein*, meaning "to attend, do service, take care of." In 1846, with the advancement of medicine, the word "therapy" shifted to mean "the science of medical treatment for disease."[77] And "disease," or "dis-ease," comes from the Old French word *desaise*, meaning "lack, want; discomfort, distress; trouble, misfortune; sickness."[78] Grief and trauma have all the components of dis-ease, and the best thing to do for discomfort is to attend to the pain, serve yourself, and find ways to heal and increase well-being.

I have participated in many types of "therapy," defined as a medical professional serving me over the course of my life, and it has often helped me to talk through my feelings with a licensed psychologist or counselor. There are many resources to find a therapist, including schools, hospitals, churches, healthcare providers, and digital databases. Seek recommendations from friends you trust. It is important to find someone you connect with who uses techniques that work for you to manage your struggles. If you aren't happy with the first person you try, don't give up. It may take a few attempts to find one you feel comfortable with. See the back of this book for a list of resources and hotlines if you are seeking therapy or need immediate medical attention.

Professional medical therapy can be useful but expensive, specifically in countries with private health care. People may not have access to a medical professional who can help. However, the beauty of positive psychology is that the theory of well-being has uncovered practices that help a person flourish in life and recognize they have the power to build positive emotion within themselves.[79] This is my ultimate goal for myself and for each of you reading this book. Seligman defines a person who is flourishing as having all the core features of well-being: positive emotions, engagement/interest, and meaning/ purpose, plus three of the six additional features: self-esteem, optimism, resilience, vitality, self-determination, and positive relationships.[80]

## Journaling

In the *Huberman Lab* podcast episode titled "A Science-Supported Journaling Protocol to Improve Mental and Physical Health,"[81] Andrew Huberman speaks about a specific journaling protocol supported by over two hundred peer-reviewed studies, originally created and researched by Dr. James Pennebaker, a professor of psychology at the University of Texas, Austin. Dr. Pennebaker found that this specific protocol helped people mentally and physically after writing about a traumatic event four times. (See the back of this book for the resource.)

This protocol asks you to write continuously for fifteen to thirty minutes in an undisturbed environment about the traumatic experience that is plaguing your body and mind. Huberman speaks about the specific instructions as follows so that each person can participate in this protocol and benefit from the same process:

> Write down your deepest emotions and thoughts as they relate to the most upsetting experience in your life. Really let go and explore your feelings and thoughts about it. As you write, you might tie this experience to your childhood, your relationship with your parents or siblings, people you have loved or loved now, or even your career or schooling. How has this experience related to who you have now become, who you have been in the past and who you would

like to become?...Write about the most dramatic or stressful experience you've ever had.[82]

It's important to note that this exercise is emotionally challenging, and you may want to give yourself time to debrief after you write it all down. And for it to be most effective, you will repeat this protocol four times and write about the exact same event each time. Huberman adds, "We are harboring these stories and experiences...of the difficult things that happen to us, and those narratives exist in our nervous system."[83] This protocol for journaling helps release these narratives from our nervous system, explained by Huberman, "[W]hen the prefrontal cortex can organize its understanding of why our autonomic nervous system was so active, well then the autonomic nervous system, it seems, becomes less likely to be active when it's not supposed to... that could at least partially explain the reductions in anxiety, the improvements in sleep, the reductions in insomnia,"[84] that different studies have proven when people practice this specific protocol. This type of journaling can improve our overall mental and physical health, especially when combined with other therapeutic practices.

## Tell Me Something Good

I play a game with my friends and family called "Tell Me Something Good" when I'm feeling down, or inundated by negative emotions internally or externally. My mom and I used to play the game when I was younger, and it helped us show appreciation for things when things felt out of control. For example, if a person is continuously complaining, their emotions are contagious, and it can increase negative feelings in the environment among others. I will ask them to "tell me something good"; this is a practical application of the positive psychology practice called "Three Blessings." Dr Seligman shares, "[P]eople tend to spend more time thinking about what is bad in life than is helpful. Worse, this focus on negative events sets us up for anxiety and depression. One way to help this from happening is to get better at thinking about and savoring what went well."[85] For the practice of Three Blessings, you set aside time every day "to write down three things that went well and why they went well."[86] This practice helps build stronger neural pathways for positive emotion. In his book *Blue Mind*, Wallace J. Nichols shares about this phenomenon:

> [N]europsychologist Rick Hanson describes in *Hardwiring Happiness: The New Brain Science of Contentment, Calm, and Confidence,* if positive experiences (1) are intense enough, (2) are novel enough, (3) occur often enough, or (4) if we direct our focused attention to them long enough, they will strengthen the brain's "happiness" neural pathways and make it easier for us to feel positive emotions.[87]

This simple and intentional practice can improve your well-being and improve your relationships.

## Gratitude Visit

At the beginning of the school year in 2022, Dr. Jeneen Graham asked the professional community to participate in an exercise from positive psychology called the "Gratitude Visit."[88] She wanted us to write a letter to someone we felt grateful for and then read it out loud to them, face to face. Dr. Seligman defines the protocol for this exercise in his book *Flourish*:

> Your task is to write a letter of gratitude to [an] individual and deliver it in person. The letter should be concrete and about three hundred words: be specific about what she did for you and how it affected your life. Let her know what you are doing now, and mention how you often remember what she did... Once you have written the testimonial, call the person and tell her you'd like to visit her...When you meet her, take your time reading the letter. Notice her reactions as well as yours...After you have read the letter (every word) discuss the content and your feelings for each other. You will be happier and less depressed one month from now.[89]

I decided to try this with my sister. I was always thanking her casually, but I had never formally shown gratitude to her in this way. And as Dr. Seligman stated, our relationship grew stronger the moment I read the letter to her. When we lose someone we love, it helps us understand the importance of personal relationships. And this is a way to cultivate positive emotion within yourself and someone else. This act of kindness ultimately improves well-being. Try it!

## Prayer and Connection

My grandmother Eileen Magni was a devout Catholic and attended church two to three times a week to connect with God and her community. My grandpa Albert "Bud" Magni would patiently sit in the pews hours after the service ended while my grandmother would go from person to person, humming quietly under her breath, to connect and pray with them. He understood the importance of her faith and her power as a prayer warrior. Our family understood my grandmother's strong connection to God through prayer and would often ask her to pray for something, knowing her faith and belief in a power greater than herself positively impacted her family, friends, and strangers alike.

When I was a child, my family prayer, (which I shared earlier in this book but will repeat again here for easy reference) was: "Lord, please bless our family. Keep us well and happy. Give us the strength, the courage, and the love to do the right thing. Through your will, Amen." The routine of this prayer brought me comfort as a child and still brings me a sense of peace as an adult when I repeat it with my daughter before bed.

To increase your sense of belonging to the whole, faith, or a belief in something bigger than yourself, does not need to align with a specific religion. Faith is personal. Anyone can tap into the power of prayer, which I believe gives you a direct connection to God. The intent to connect is more powerful than the words you say. I pray silently in my head throughout the day, and I speak the words out loud when it feels right. I repeat the Lord's Prayer in times of anxiety to help me fall asleep, or the Serenity Prayer when I need patience. I text prayers to my friends when they need strength to heal. I pray for my family, my friends, and strangers alike, just like my grandmother modeled for me. I pray in gratitude when I am in nature and when I see something that makes me feel awe. I giggle and emphatically say "Thank you, Jesus!", copying Brett's granny, every time I find a parking spot. Prayer fills me with hope and thankfulness, which are two things that feel really good. Try it!

## Medication

Thankfully, the use of medication for mental health seems to have become normalized, with more and more of the population feeling comfortable talking openly about their usage of it. As I wrote about earlier in this book, I too have been medicated in the past for anxiety and depression, and I know the value of it. When I have an asthma attack, I take a rescue inhaler. When I have a psyche attack, I can take a rescue medicine, whether short-term anti-anxiety medication, long-term antidepressant medication, or a combination of the two.

Even just having this anti-anxiety medicine in my possession during the first few years of grief helped me to stay calmer. I knew I had a safety net to catch me, which made it easier to take one step forward at a time, knowing it was okay if I tripped and fell. This safety net was crucial for me and still is, especially as a last resort. You can do all the things I have suggested in this book and more, and still not feel the benefits of healing. It is so important to recognize when you need more help and to seek it as soon as possible.

## September 2023, Age 42

"Doctor, so I'm doing all the things to make myself feel better, and nothing is working. I am feeling really overwhelmed and irritated often throughout the day, to the point of tears." I wiped my eyes with a tissue.

"Have you tried exercising?"

"Yes, every day, for at least an hour. Running, spinning, yoga..." I trailed off.

"How about your diet?"

"Well, I have a lot of food restrictions due to allergies, so I eat very clean, unprocessed, real food."

"Do you drink alcohol?"

"Yes, limited in social situations, but I stopped six weeks ago to see if it would help me sleep and feel better," I reported.

"How's your sleep? What do you do to relax?"

"Not great. I fall asleep quickly, but then I wake up and can't go back to sleep. I bought a jacuzzi as a COVID purchase," I giggled, still teary, "and I sit in it in the morning when I wake up and in the evening before I go to bed."

"Okay, great, what about meditation?"

"Yes," I laughed, surprised he was asking. "I do the Balance app meditations every day. I even practice the Wim Hof breathing method regularly to release feel-good neurotransmitters."

He looked at me concerned, maybe because I used the word "neurotransmitters."

"Well, have you tried praying? When was the last time you went to church?"

I started to cry again. "Look, I really appreciate everything that you are asking me," I kindly encouraged him. "And yes, I need to go to church more often. My daughter's sports schedule has made it difficult to attend regularly," I admitted, feeling the shame of judgment. "But I pray every day. I know you are trying to get to the source of the problem, and I wish I could tell you what it is. All I know is that I'm *NOT okay*, even after doing all these things to feel better. I keep it together at work, but when I get home, I turn into 'monster mom' and 'lousy wife.'" (These nicknames I gave myself were a running narrative of negative self-talk in my head that grew louder when I felt overwhelmed and impatient.) "I am so short-tempered and anxious. I am crying and losing it over nothing. I need help."

"Okay, well I appreciate your determination to try to help yourself," the doctor said, "and it sounds like maybe an antidepressant might help you. What do you think?"

"Yes," I gratefully agreed. "I have been on them before, and I think I need something just to take the edge off. I would love to try the lowest dose possible. Maybe if it helps me get down to a level 2 or 3 instead of a 10, that would be wonderful."

"Sure, let's try it for six months and see. Sometimes just knowing you are taking something gives people a greater sense of control over their anxiety."

"Thank you, I really appreciate it."

This conversation was frustrating, and it took all my determination and persistence to continue to advocate for myself when I felt so helpless and weak. The entire time I wanted to scream, "Please help me!" I felt frustrated with my own lack of control over my mind and body, but I did my best to respond, through tears, knowing the doctor had good intentions. Sometimes medication is the answer, and that is fantastic if it makes you feel better. There is no shame in getting help and medicating to reach a balanced mental state.

Medical doctors will advise you on the many different choices for medication, including antidepressants and anti-anxiety medication. Each medication affects people differently, and they may cause side effects, so it is important to consult with a medical doctor and be monitored closely when starting a new medication. Please seek professional help for any issues that come up when using a new medication. I like to keep a daily journal through my WHOOP activity tracker to closely monitor my health metrics and mood and catch any significant changes that occur from taking the medication. If the medicine makes me feel worse, I am proactive in communicating with my doctor to find something else or a different dosage that works for my body.

## Space and Grace

When grief entered my life, I worked myself to the bone because I chose to move too much and too often. My mind refused to rest, and physical distractions from my thoughts were easier to manage. The movement created the feel-good neurotransmitters in my body, and I was addicted to them. But that wasn't healthy either. I needed to move in moderation, learning how to rest and sit still with my grief.

Some days, almost ten years after my grief started when Brett was diagnosed with cancer, I still feel the need to run as hard as I can until my body says to stop. And some days I choose to sit in the jacuzzi. I have learned to give myself space and grace for either choice: whether I hurt myself running ten miles because my demons won't let me stop until I am completely exhausted, or I sit and "do nothing" in the jacuzzi. It's important to note that my perception of "doing nothing" when I'm resting is a testament to my old self-perception that if I rest, I'm being lazy. I have come to realize the value of rest, and I continue to remind myself to release judgment when I feel like I'm "doing nothing." We get stronger when we balance work and rest.

Do what you feel you need, not want, based on your awareness of your own body and mind. Allow the space and grace for understanding how you feel or what you think, without judgment. In his book *Untethered Soul: The Journey Beyond Yourself,* Michael A. Singer illustrates this idea of space in his belief about the distinct separation of our soul from our feelings and emotions. He states, "You are not the pain you feel, nor are you the part that periodically stresses out. None of these disturbances have anything to do with you. You are the one who notices these things...you can simply permit these disturbances to come up, and you can let them go."[90] Grief makes you oscillate from feeling completely numb to feeling all the feels at the same time. It is a fascinating phenomenon. If you experience these waves, notice and welcome them. Jump on your board and enjoy the ride! And when the wave passes, let it go. Grieving also allows your body to do what it needs to do to heal. If you need to cry, then cry. If you need to throw or hurt something to get out your anger, choose a nonliving object that doesn't feel pain. Tap into the power of grief for your body and mind. If you need to sit on the floor of your kitchen and sob like a baby, do it. I did, and I promise I felt better afterward. Then, get up and move. If you need therapy or medication, or a combination of both, get it. I did, and I felt better as a result.

These are the essential practices that work for me. I hope you try them and others to find passion in movement, meditation, and breathwork, and please seek further help through therapeutic practices and/or medication, if needed. Please connect with me to share what works for you—I can't wait to learn more!

# Keep Going

So, what's next?

This book is an intentional continuation of an act of service. I am increasing my scope of positive impact to help others through understanding, comfort, awareness, education, connection, and the essential practices to thrive.

We often consider our lives in body and mind to have a linear trajectory toward death. We are born with the vitality of youth; culturally, we believe children have the greatest natural capacity to move and learn with great flexibility and curiosity. As we age, the movement and learning tend to diminish, and our bodies and minds become increasingly rigid.

However, our life, in mind and body, does not have to follow this linear descent toward death. We can choose to live each day by making a positive choice. That choice will feel good, which will generate more positive choices. This cycle creates healthy habits and gives us the momentum to live life to the fullest. We are not guaranteed tomorrow, so why wouldn't we choose to live each day to our greatest capacity and perpetuate potential?

In his book *The Pursuit of Happiness*, David Myers lists ten things that are important to thrive:

- Realize that enduring happiness doesn't come from success.
- Take control of your time.
- Act happy.
- Seek work and leisure that engages your skills.
- Join the "movement" movement.
- Give your body the sleep it wants.
- Give priority to close relationships.
- Focus beyond the self.
- Keep a gratitude journal.
- Nurture your spiritual self.[91]

I love this list, and I would love to finish my book (and my life) with a happy ending, to wrap it up in a beautiful shiny golden bow like all the rom-coms I love to watch. But happiness is fleeting. Instead of pretending that you will achieve never-ending happiness and live forever after reading this book, my hope is that you mindfully live for today with the intention to positively impact tomorrow. Living is an action, and it's subjective. One can physically be alive, with all body systems working, but choose to be solitary and stationary in mind and body—characteristics of the dead. In contrast, from my experience watching Brett fully *live* the last two years of his life, one can be dying and choose to move, continue to learn, and connect with and serve others daily to find peace and joy when they pass on.

I hope you find peace knowing you will feel moments of happiness, sadness, and all the things in between in this life— and, thanks to grief, probably all at the same time. That's fantastic. My hope is that you move, meditate, breathe, and connect with others in a way that serves you and them for ultimate health today and all the days after.

Also, for guidance and inspirational purposes, I will share my own personal intentions with you as a template if you are feeling lost. Through all the feels I experience daily:

- I will tap into the "big-win energy" of essential practices and will choose to move, meditate, and breathe in a way that serves me to live each day to its fullest.
- I will connect with the community that continues to empower me to grow and serve others.
- I will choose to feel moments of joy and gratitude every day, no matter the circumstances.
- I will continue to embrace grief. By giving it a huge welcoming hug, I allow the power of connection to heal me and others.

The activities in this book and final intentions are specific to my own experience. It doesn't necessarily matter how you choose to achieve these things or if your intentions are the same as mine. My hope is that some of these intentions and reflections resonate with you and that you are inspired to create and achieve your own intentions unique to your experience for healing, growth, and connection.

The most important aspect of this book is the **intention to keep going**:

- To live each day with a sense of love and curiosity for yourself, for others, and for the world around you
- To help you heal and connect with others to improve your relationships and make a positive impact while you are alive

When grief comes knocking at your door, for whatever reason, it is vital to remember that you can let it in. As Mallika Chopra so beautifully explains:

> Change doesn't happen when we feel confident, strong and rooted. The blessing of uncertainty is that it gives us the nudge we need to dig deep—to incubate and reflect on what we want—and to find the courage to carve out a different path.[92]

It's going to hurt, but embrace it, and do what you can to take the next step forward. One step at a time and one moment at a time, give yourself grace to listen to your body. Some moments, you'll sit alone in stillness and sadness— and breathe. Some moments, you'll move and connect with others—and breathe. All are important aspects for healing, growth, and strength. Just remember in all that you do, continue to breathe—not in the reflexive way that we all do inherently thanks to our medulla oblongata,[93] but with intentionality in a way that is life-giving. Your breath is your greatest strength.

If you are an athlete or a former athlete, remember the "athlete grind" to work harder to get results isn't always the answer. In swimming, when you work harder and fight the water, the water wins. It will fatigue you to exhaustion. The natural power of water is stronger than human bodies. But if you *use* the water, by tapping into its power and strength, you become the water. It moves you...and you become stronger. Work smarter, not harder, in your athletic endeavors and your transition out of them. Educate yourself on grief and loss. Everyone will experience it at some point in their lives. You may experience it sooner with a loss of identity, social athletic community, and/or loss of a productive daily routine from athletics.

The belief that you can "beat grief" by pushing it away and fighting it through distraction and denial only increases the time you are stuck in it, "underwater." Just like water, grief can drown you. You can't fight against it. When you lean into grief and become aware of its power to heal and restore you through shared connection, it helps you swim to the surface and become stronger.

If you find yourself hiding in your own bear's den due to grief, trauma, the culmination of athletic pursuits, or suffering from disillusionment or depression, you are not alone. When you're ready to stop hibernating, we will be here for you. Please seek help. When you ask for help (as hard as it is for most of us), and you're willing to receive help, you inevitably help others too. We all feel the need to be needed in this life. Acts of service nourish our souls, both when we receive them and when we perform them. When you ask for help, you allow someone else to feel needed and implicitly make them feel better too. This is the beauty of human connection, and it's a miraculous thing when it's reciprocated.

Please connect with me for more. There is so much more to come. More words of impact, more connections, more shared soup, more healing...

When the door is shut and the story ends, look to the window. You will find a new perspective through the panes of glass. When the air calls to you, open it up, spread your wings, and create expansion for a new story to begin. I can't wait to hear about your adventures and thank you for joining me on mine. I am forever grateful and inspired by your courage to grieve, connect, and fly. Let's dance together like hummingbirds.

# Acknowledgments

*"Our most powerful form of motivation is a collective, rather than a personal cause. A cause fuelled by our sense of belonging."*

—Owen Eastwood, *Belonging*[94]

The completion of this book fills me with a sense of joy—not only for the intention to share all the goodness from hardship that I have felt in my life, but also for the ability to create something with others that will leave a lasting impact on *you*. I am grateful that you completed this adventure with me and experienced the power of shared stories and human connection. We belong. I acknowledge with gratitude YOU, the reader, for your interest in my story. You have increased your knowledge of the sacred dance of well-being. And I acknowledge with gratitude your ability to share this book with others and share your own story. There is power in a shared language around grief and trauma. We make each other better.

Thank you to my family, whose love for words, artistic creativity, and passion to dance have inspired me and contributed to this art. Lish, thank you for encouraging and supporting me all the time, especially when the gremlins of worry and doubt crept into my thoughts. Thank you to Samantha Ramsden (Winfield) for your beautiful artistic interpretations of this book through your thoughtful illustrations. Your attention to detail is immaculate, and your drawings are stunning. They make me feel a sense of power and peace, and I revel in the existence of both simultaneously in your art.

Thank you to my mentors, professors, and teachers throughout my life at Carlsbad High School, UC Berkeley, Concordia University, Irvine, MindfulSchools.org, and St. Margaret's Episcopal School. You have guided me to grow and flourish. Thank you to Mr. Beauvais, my AP high school English teacher whose passion for Shakespeare, poetry, and prose sparked in me a sense of belonging to the lovers of words. Thank you to my swimming coaches, Dave Salo, Teri McKeever, and Milt Nelms, for your belief and support of my athletic dreams, helping me build strength and resilience, and introducing me to yoga and breathwork. Thank you to all the yoga teachers who have influenced me to listen to my body with grace and love—from the very beginning, Devin Wicks, who shared his love of dance and Savasana with us at Cal, to all the wonderful teachers at CorePower Yoga: Shawna Wo, Robin Gallo, Wendy Black,

Nassim A, Danica Bl, Kaitlin D, Candice Bourgeois, and more. The light and darkness in me honors the light and darkness in you...Namaste.

With utmost gratitude, I thank Mallika Chopra for sharing her wisdom and experience of intention and meditation, and taking the time to connect with me and countless others. You poured water and sunlight into my heart that harbored the seed of intention for this book. I had no idea how this intention would manifest at the time, and I am in awe of the growth that occurred to create this book by opening myself up and writing down a clear intention, as you suggested. Also, I owe sincere gratitude to the scientists, professors, practitioners, and writers of positive psychology. Thank you to Dr. Jeneen Graham for sharing Dr. Martin E.P. Seligman's book *Flourish* with me. Thank you to Dr. Seligman and Dr. Robert Tedeschi for your dedication to research, data, and the sharing of knowledge to help people understand how to cultivate well-being and grow from trauma. I look forward to pursuing more knowledge in this field of study because of your inspiring work and shared love for humanity's well-being.

Thank you to Danielle McDonough, who introduced me to Jake Kelfer and his company Big Idea to Best Seller (BIB). Thank you to the entire team at BIB: Jake Kelfer, Mikey Kershisnik, Anastasia Voll, Teresa Miller, and the cover design team behind the scenes. Jake, your energy and passion to help people publish their books is remarkable. Thank you for your belief in your team and what felt like your blind faith in my ability to produce something meaningful. From our initial phone call, I was energized to see this project to completion. I am grateful for your intention to serve others. Mikey, you are an amazing project manager! Thank you for your enthusiasm, radiant smile, and ability to connect me with an incredible team of people. I felt comfort trusting your ability to help bring this vision to life. It was such a pleasure to connect with you, learn from your wisdom about the publishing process, and receive guidance about what to include in this book. I had no idea how to get my ideas to print, and you made the process seamless and enjoyable. Anastasia, I cherish our time together and growing friendship through laughter in our weekly check-ins. Your initial guiding questions, invaluable knowledge of the writing process, and immense support made this book better. Teresa, thank you for your incredible attention to detail when editing this book. Your skills are awe-inspiring! I am grateful knowing you cared about the quality of this book as much as I do. I hope you all feel the joy that I feel, holding the real thing in your hands, knowing your contributions were integral to the quality and impact of this book to serve others.

In the final stages of this book, as I began to share it with others for feedback and reflection, I felt a higher vibration of energy and the power of connection and collaboration.

Thank you to Heather Petri, not only for your unconditional love, understanding, and friendship, but also for your power to connect others and bring them into your infinite circle of belonging. You cast your net wide with your love for humans, and you attract incredibly powerful people. Thank you for inviting me to Berkeley to speak at the 2024 NCAA Women's Water Polo Championships about "Big Win Energy,"[95] which organically connected me with Erin Cafaro, Dr. Lenny Weirsma, and the Starretts. I loved all of our conversations about athletic transition and intention to improve this community through education, connection, and care. Thank you to Dr. Kelly Starrett and Juliet Starrett, who expressed support and excitement for this book because of their shared interest in human performance and vitality both mentally and physically. Kelly, I was inspired by your book recommendation, *Belonging* by Owen Eastwood, which ultimately brought to light the meaning of human connection that I have always felt but couldn't explain. I look forward to more adventures together and intend to contribute to the powerful community you have created serving others.

Thank you to Naoko Watanabe, Adam Lee, Erin Cafaro, Dr. Lenny Weirsma, Gina Tucci-Karsinovas, and Tyler Hawkins for your dedication to helping athletes transition and thrive in their next endeavors through your education and research. Thank you all for helping me ideate the transition for more, beyond the book, to "keep going" as a tribe.

Thank you to all the powerful mermaids and watermen in my life who helped me find the surface when things grew dark, and continue to inspire me to dance: Kyla Winfield, Alisha Charlemagne, Randy and Michele Waier, John Winfield, Heather Petri, Dave Denniston, Naoko Watanabe, Lexie Kelley, Kristy Kowal, Erika "Monkey" Lorenz, Susan Helmrich, Misty Hyman, Rada Owen, Mermaid Flower, Aaron Peirsol, and all the lovers of water. Your combined love and strength make this world a better place.

My heartfelt thanks and acknowledgment of all those who personally shared in this story of the love and loss of Brett Winfield. He touched so many lives, and we all felt the loss when heaven gained his immaculate spirit. To the BFSU crew: Aaron Clousing, Luke Wright, Ashley Cunnane, Rachel Ridgeway, Lara Pease, Erin Coffman, Trent Calder, and Lauren Calder, thank you for your love and laughter during challenging times. I am eternally grateful for your friendship.

And to my grief-widow wives, Pharaba and Tricia: I couldn't walk this path without you. Thank you. I love you.

Jay, thank you for your love and support of Kyla and me. Your presence in our lives has allowed me to grow and expand, feeling your love and understanding of all the light and darkness I bring with me into our relationship. Thank you for embracing it all. I love you.

Kyla, when the time is right and you have read this book to completion, you will understand the love and compassion I have for you as a mom and as a human. I am grateful and honored to be your mom. We are all human, and we belong to something bigger than ourselves. In gratitude, I cherish that our arms are forever linked in a chain of love. Our bond is eternal. Those who came before you are smiling down on your life while the sun is shining on you. I will continue to cheer you on as you make your own story and positively impact this world. Keep going...I love you forever.

# Resources

**Hotlines**

National Suicide Prevention Lifeline: 1-800-273-8255

Depression and Bipolar Support Alliance: Text DBSA to 741-741

International Association for Suicide Prevention: findahelpline.com/i/iasp

Substance Abuse and Mental Health Services Admin: 1-800-662-HELP (4357)

**Big Win Energy**

bigwinenergy.org

**Grief**

Hot Young Widows Club Grief Resources : hotyoungwidowsclub.com/general-resources

Dammit Doll: dammitdolls.com

Griefshare: griefshare.org

## Breathing Techniques

What Breath Does to Your Brain: greatergood.berkeley.edu/article/item/what_focusing_on_the_breath_does_to_your_brain

Data on Breath Connection to Brain: journals.physiology.org/doi/full/10.1152/jn.00551.2017

How to Fight Stress with Intentional Breathing: mindful.org/fight-stress-intentional-breathing/

Deepak Chopra Daily Breath Podcast: podcasts.apple.com/us/podcast/daily-breath-with-deepak-chopra/id1458887650

Wim Hof Guided Breathing Exercise: youtube.com/watch?v=tybOi4hjZFQ

The Power and Mysticism of Ujjayi Pranayama: ashramyoga.com/single-post/ujjayi

Box-Breathing Technique: webmd.com/balance/what-is-box-breathing

Diaphragmatic (Belly) Breathing: health.harvard.edu/healthbeat/learning-diaphragmatic-breathing

Nasal Breathing Benefits Research: journals.physiology.org/doi/full/10.1152/ajpregu.00148.2023

Deep-Breathing Exercises: positivepsychology.com/deep-breathing-techniques-exercises/

## Body Scan

Body Scan Meditation for Beginners: health.clevelandclinic.org/body-scan-meditation

**Mindfulness and Meditation**

The Science of Mindfulness: mindful.org/the-science-of-mindfulness

Mindfulness for Grief and Loss: mindful.org/mindfulness-for-grief-and-loss

Mental Health Worksheets: positivepsychology.com/mental-health-activities-worksheets-books

Emotional Well-Being: positivepsychology.com/emotional-health-activities

**Movement and Mobility**

Five-Minute Happiness Break: greatergood.berkeley.edu/podcasts/item/happiness_break_a_walking_meditation_with_dan_harris_of_10_happier

The Ready State: thereadystate.com

**The Power of Connection**

A Meditation on Interconnectedness: greatergood.berkeley.edu/podcasts/item/happiness_break_pilina_hawaiian_connection_with_jo_qinaau

Seven Ingredients to Thrive: viacharacter.org/topics/articles/you-need-these-7-things-to-thrive-research-says

*The Pursuit of Happiness* by David Myers: davidmyers.org/books/the-pursuit-of-happiness/suggestions

*Belonging: The Ancient Code of Togetherness* by Owen Eastwood: amazon.com/Belonging-Owen-Eastwood/dp/1529415063

**Athletic Performance/Transition Resources**

Beyond the Scoreboards, Gina Tucci (Karsinovas): beyondthescoreboards.com

Pelorus, CEO Tyler Hawkins (high school athletic development resilience and leadership training): youtube.com/watch?v=nes8WACpXNg

# About the Author

Staciana Winfield is a motivational speaker and performance coach, a 2000 Olympic gold medalist, and a five-time American Record holder. She speaks on how to cope with the grief of losing a loved one, as well as how athletes can transition after sport in a healthy and safe way to increase well-being through positive psychology practices. In addition to speaking, she teaches physiology, health, and physical education at St. Margaret's Episcopal School in San Juan Capistrano, California, and is head coach of both their men's and women's swim teams.

From 2000 to 2004, she swam at UC Berkeley, winning fourteen All-American titles in addition to her Olympic gold—all while earning her bachelor of science degree in social psychology of sport. She earned her master of arts in coaching and athletic administration from Concordia University, Irvine, as well as certifications in mindfulness and Pilates.

Since the age of twelve, Staciana has had alopecia universalis, an autoimmune disease that causes hair loss. She is a spokesperson for raising awareness of the autoimmune disorder and has worked with the Children's Alopecia Project, helping younger children with alopecia understand what it's like to enjoy life with the condition as a kid, a teenager, and an adult.

You can contact Staciana via her website: bigwinenergy.org.

# Endnotes

1    Wallace J. Nichols, *Blue Mind: The Surprising Science That Shows How Being Near, In, On, or Under Water Can Make You Happier, Healthier, More Connected, and Better at What You Do* (New York: Back Bay Books, 2015) 248-49.

2    Owen Eastwood, *Belonging: Unlock Your Potential with the Ancient Code of Togetherness* (New York: Quercus, 2021), 20.

3    Quoted in Martin E.P. Seligman, *Flourish: A Visionary New Understanding of Happiness and Well-being*, (New York: Atria Paperback, 2011), 131.

4    Quoted in Mallika Chopra, *Living with Intent: My Somewhat Messy Journey to Purpose, Peace, and Joy* (New York: Harmony Books, 2015), 118.

5    lululemon athletica, "Our Manifesto," accessed June 5, 2024, https://www.lululemon.fr/en-fr/c/community/about-us/our-manifesto.

6    Nora McInerny is the of author of *The Hot Young Widows Club* (New York: Simon & Schuster/TED, 2019) and runs a resource website of the same name. More information is available at hotyoungwidowsclub.com.

7    Inspired by David Cunningham, Elevate Forward Now, LLC, A.I.R. retreat, Bodega Bay, California, April 14, 2024.

8    Owen Eastwood, *Belonging*, 5.

9    Owen Eastwood, *Belonging*, 16.

10    Andrew Huberman, "A Science-Supported Journaling Protocol to Improve Mental and Physical Health," November 20, 2023, in *Huberman Lab*, podcast, 00:23:11, https://www.hubermanlab.com/episode/a-science-supported-journaling-protocol-to-improve-mental-physical-health.

11    Coleman Barks, *The Essential Rumi* (San Francisco: HarperOne, 2004), 122.

12    Milky Chance, "Stolen Dance," released June 20, 2014, track 11 on *Sadnecessary*, Republic Records.

13      Milky Chance, "Stolen Dance."

14      Milky Chance, "Stolen Dance."

15      M.K., *The Big Book of Rumi Quotes* (Independently published, 2023), https://www.amazon.com/Big-Book-Rumi-Quotes/dp/B0C1J2N5JB/, 170.

16      Coleman Barks, *The Essential Rumi*, 32.

17      Wallace J. Nichols, *Blue Mind*, 267.

18      Wallace J. Nichols, *Blue Mind*, 11.

19      Coleman Barks, *The Essential Rumi*, 20.

20      Richard Magill and David Anderson, *Motor Learning and Control: Concepts and Applications*, 10th ed. (McGraw-Hill: New York, 2014), 32.

21      Martin E.P. Seligman, *Flourish*, 11.

22      John Lennon, "Imagine," recorded 1971, track 1 on *Imagine*, Apple Records.

23      John Lennon, "Imagine."

24      David Hamilton, "Real vs Imaginary in the Brain and Body" (blog), February 19, 2019, https://drdavidhamilton.com/real-vs-imaginary-in-the-brain-and-body/.

25      Owen Eastwood, *Belonging*, 144.

26      ABBA, "Dancing Queen," recorded 1975, track 2 on *Arrival*, Polar.

27      Owen Eastwood, *Belonging*, 115, quoting Robert Sapolsky, *Behave* (2017, Penguin Random House), 70.

28      Oliver Goldsmith, *The Citizen of the World; or, Letters from a Chinese Philosopher, Residing in London, to His Friends in the East*, (Dublin, Ireland: Printed for George and Alex Ewing, 1762), 29, https://quod.lib.umich.edu/cgi/t/text/text-idx?c=ecco;cc=ecco;rgn=main;view=text;idno=004776950.0001.001.

29      Coleman Barks, *The Essential Rumi*, 307.

30      Nine Inch Nails, "Closer," released 1994, track 5 on *The Downward Spiral*, Nothing Records.

31      Beth-Sarah Wright, *Dignity: Seven Strategies for Creating Authentic Community* (New York: Church Publishing, 2020).

32      Nine Inch Nails, "Closer."

33      Ludacris, "Move Bitch (feat. Mystikal and I-20)," recorded 2001, track 10 on *Word of Mouf*, Disturbing tha Peace, Def Jam South.

34      Milky Chance, "Stolen Dance."

35      Milky Chance, "Stolen Dance."

36      Milky Chance, "Stolen Dance."

37      Milky Chance, "Stolen Dance."

38      Coleman Barks, *The Essential Rumi*, 122.

39      "Tear Soup," reprinted with permission from Grief Watch, griefwatch.com, copyright 1999 and 2011, all rights reserved.

40      More information is available at griefshare.org.

41      lululemon athletica, "Our Manifesto," https://www.lululemon.fr/en-fr/c/community/about-us/our-manifesto.

42      Nora McInerny, "We Don't 'Move On' from Grief. We Move Forward with It.," TED Talks, video, Nov. 2018, 14:50, https://www.ted.com/talks/nora_mcinerny_we_don_t_move_on_from_grief_we_move_forward_with_it.

43      Nora McInerny, "We Don't 'Move On.'"

44      Nora McInerny, "We Don't 'Move On.'"

45      Martin E.P. Seligman, *Flourish*, 155.

46      David Hamilton, "Real vs Imaginary."

47      Daniela Ramirez-Duran, "Exploring the Mind–Body Connection through Research," PositivePsychology.com, Sept. 16, 2020, https://positivepsychology.com/mind-body-connection/.

48      David Berceli et al., "Effects of Self-induced Unclassified Therapeutic Tremors on Quality of Life among Non-professional Caregivers: A Pilot Study," *Global Advances in Health and Medicine* 3, no. 5 (Sept. 2014): 45–48, https://www.ncbi.nlm.nih.gov/pmc/articles/PMC4268601/.

49    Martin E.P. Seligman, *Flourish*, 159.

50    Martin E.P. Seligman, *Flourish*, 126.

51    Martin E.P. Seligman, *Flourish*, 161.

52    Martin E.P. Seligman, *Flourish*, 162.

53    Owen Eastwood, *Belonging*, 22.

54    Owen Eastwood, *Belonging*, 23.

55    Owen Eastwood, *Belonging*, 106.

56    Owen Eastwood, *Belonging*, 144.

57    Owen Eastwood, *Belonging*, 20.

58    Owen Eastwood, *Belonging*, 19.

59    Staciana Winfield, bigwinenergy.org, 2024.

60    Daniela Ramirez-Duran, "Exploring the Mind–Body Connection."

61    Daniela Ramirez-Duran, "Exploring the Mind–Body Connection."

62    Daniela Ramirez-Duran, "Exploring the Mind–Body Connection."

63    Ana Gotter, "7 Science-Backed Benefits of Pranayama," Healthline, March 22, 2023, https://www.healthline.com/health/pranayama-benefits#bottom-line.

64    Peter Attia, *Outlive: The Science and Art of Longevity* (New York: Harmony Books, 2023), 10.

65    Peter Attia, *Outlive*, 10.

66    Peter Attia, *Outlive*, 11.

67    Peter Attia, *Outlive*, 11.

68    Peter Attia, *Outlive*, 217.

69    Peter Attia, *Outlive*, 218.

70    Peter Attia, *Outlive*, 225.

71      Mallika Chopra, "Parent-Up" speech, St. Margaret's Episcopal School, San Juan Capistrano, January 24, 2020.

72      Mallika Chopra, *Living with Intent*, 63.

73      Mallika Chopra, *Living with Intent*, 66.

74      Mallika Chopra, *Living with Intent*, 113.

75      Cleveland Clinic, "Body Scan Meditation for Beginners: How to Make the Mind/Body Connection," Feb. 2, 2023, https://health.clevelandclinic.org/body-scan-meditation.

76      Can Wang et al., "Extracurricular Sports Activities Modify the Proprioceptive Map in Children Aged 5–8 Years," *Scientific Reports* 12 (2022): 9338, https://www.ncbi.nlm.nih.gov/pmc/articles/PMC9167298/.

77      "Therapy (n.)," Etymonline, https://www.etymonline.com/word/therapy.

78      "Disease (n.)," Etymonline, https://www.etymonline.com/search?q=disease.

79      Martin E.P. Seligman, *Flourish*, 141.

80      Martin E.P. Seligman, *Flourish*, 27.

81      Andrew Huberman, "A Science-Supported Journaling Protocol," 0:00:33.

82      Andrew Huberman, "A Science-Supported Journaling Protocol," 00:12:47.

83      Andrew Huberman, "A Science-Supported Journaling Protocol," 00:22:07.

84      Andrew Huberman, "A Science-Supported Journaling Protocol," 01:22:51.

85      Martin E.P. Seligman, *Flourish*, 33.

86      Martin E.P. Seligman, *Flourish*, 33.

87      Wallace J. Nichols, *Blue Mind*, 58-59.

88      Martin E.P. Seligman, *Flourish*, 30.

89      Martin E.P. Seligman, *Flourish*, 30.

90       Michael A. Singer, *The Untethered Soul: The Journey Beyond Yourself* (Oakland: New Harbinger Publications and Noetic Books, 2007), 85.

91       David G. Myers, "Want a Happier Life?," accessed June 5, 2024, https://davidmyers.org/books/the-pursuit-of-happiness/suggestions.

92       Mallika Chopra, *Living with Intent*, 51.

93       Keiko Ikeda et al., "The Respiratory Control Mechanisms in the Brainstem and Spinal Cord: Integrative Views of the Neuroanatomy and Neurophysiology," introduction, *The Journal of Physiological Sciences* 67, no. 1 (Aug. 2016): 45–62, https://www.ncbi.nlm.nih.gov/pmc/articles/PMC5368202/#:~:text=The%20respiratory%20center%20is%20located,homogeneous%20population%20of%20pacemaker%20cells.

94       Owen Eastwood, *Belonging*, 102.

95       Staciana Winfield, bigwinenergy.org, 2024.

Made in the USA
Las Vegas, NV
15 August 2024

93915130R00194